Poole

THE NEW RULES OF NETWORKING

THE ESSENTIAL RULES AND SECRETS TO MODERN NETWORKING

Rob Yeung

Copyright © 2006 Rob Yeung

This book was first published as *The Rules of Networking*
This edition published in 2012 by Marshall Cavendish Business
An imprint of Marshall Cavendish International

1 New Industrial Road, Singapore 536196
genrefsales@sg.marshallcavendish.com
www.marshallcavendish.com/genref

Other Marshall Cavendish offices: Marshall Cavendish Corporation. 99 White
Plains Road, Tarrytown NY 10591-9001, USA • Marshall Cavendish International
(Thailand) Co Ltd. 253 Asoke, 12th Flr, Sukhumvit 21 Road, Klongtoey Nua,
Wattana, Bangkok 10110, Thailand • Marshall Cavendish (Malaysia) Sdn Bhd.
Times Subang, Lot 46, Subang Hi-Tech Industrial Park, Batu Tiga, 40000 Shah Alam,
Selangor Darul Ehsan, Malaysia

Marshall Cavendish is a trademark of Times Publishing Limited

The right of Rob Yeung to be identified as the author of this work has been asserted by
him in accordance with the Copyright, Designs and Patents Act 1988.

A CIP record for this book is available from the British Library

ISBN 978-981-4382-31-1

Printed in Singapore by Fabulous Printers Pte Ltd

Contents

Foreword

Working life ain't simple any more. There was a time when you worked hard, your employer looked after you, and you just carried on until you received your gold carriage clock on retirement. But that simple career path is dead. There are more threats in the world – mergers and acquisitions, globalization and jobs being outsourced or offshored, downsizing programs, and job cuts. And these have turned the workplace into a minefield of treacherous personalities, unexploded resentments, and ticking egos. Who can you really trust? What do you need to do or say to get ahead?

But there are more opportunities too. You aren't tied to the one employer any more – you can move around and seek bigger pay rises, greater responsibility, more interesting challenges. Employers no longer look down on people who want to take career breaks to go traveling or do something different. You can go freelance or set up your own business and try to make your first million. The world is literally your oyster.

In this complex world of work, the rules of work have changed. We can all think of people who got promoted who didn't deserve to be. Come to think of it, we can all probably think of someone who does deserve to get promoted, but hasn't been. And, to add insult to injury, on top of our day-to-day jobs, we're expected to deal with office politics, to be a good team player, and to network. And how do you get headhunted exactly? All of these are things that no one ever really tells you how to do.

Well, this series tells you how to do these things. And this book looks at networking – probably the most important single skill that everybody talks about, but no one ever teaches you.

Most people throw up their hands in horror at even the mention of the word. It conjures up images of having to fawn and be insincere to people you don't like in order to get ahead. However, I'm going to show you that the reality is much more civilized. No matter how uncomfortable or awkward you may feel about meeting strangers, networking is a skill that can be learnt.

But let's cut to the chase. After all, who has the time to sit and read hefty management tomes? Too often, an author has a handful of great ideas, but then ruins them by spending hundreds and hundreds of pages explaining them carefully in excruciating detail, giving too much background and yawn, yawn, yawn…. I've lost the will to live.

When I read one of those books, I start to flick through the chapters and pages with increasing impatience – wanting to shout, "Come on, get to the point!" Ah, but there is a reason why so many books are so long. The truth of the matter is that many publishers want their authors to write lengthy books so that they can slap on a big fat cover price. So this book is short and full of practical, pithy advice.

This book will not patronize or talk down to you. It is not a guide for idiots or dummies. You are a bright professional who simply wants some new ideas and nuggets of information. You do not need everything spelt out for you with endless examples to get the point across.

So if you have ever wanted to know how to get ahead in your career – but don't have the time to plough through Bible-sized manuals or books that talk down to you – then this is the book for you. Feel free to flick through and find the chapters that are most interesting for you.

Finally, if you have any fantastic networking tips or stories that you'd like to share with the world – drop me an email. I'll shove it in the second edition and you'll get your name in print!

Rob Yeung
rob@talentspace.co.uk

Introduction: Six Scenarios

Let's get something straight right away. Networking is not just for salespeople. Sure, if you work in sales, then networking is a critical tool for finding customers and clients. But for the rest of us, networking is still vital if you can answer "yes" to any one of the following questions:

1 Would you like to get promoted?
2 Do you want to earn more money?
3 Would you like to get offered a new job?
4 Do you work for yourself as a freelancer or consultant?
5 Are you a part of an organization that wants to succeed?
6 Have you aspirations of working for yourself in the future?

If the answer to any one of these is "yes," then you'd better get networking.

Let's take each of these questions in turn:

1 Would you like to get promoted?

You have probably had the sneaking suspicion – or maybe you already know for a fact – that the wrong sorts of people seem to be getting promoted. If you think about it, it often seems to be the people who schmooze with managers and talk up their achievements. They aren't any better at the job than you are, but they create the impression that they are. They get noticed. And consequently, they get promoted.

It's not fair, it's not right. But if you want to chase a promotion, then you had better start to work on building your profile too. You may not agree with the ways that they get themselves noticed – terms such as "brown nosing," "sucking up," "kissing up," and so on litter the corporate landscape to describe their behavior.

But just because there are bad ways to generate a profile does not mean that there are not perfectly good ways too. Asking people to input into your development and seeking a mentor are just two examples of how networking can help you move forwards in your career. Keeping in touch with acquaintances in competitor organizations can help you to get one up on them too.

Just as one example, the UK's fastest growing law firm Eversheds explicitly refers to network.ing – both internally across regional offices and externally with clients – as a specific skill that senior lawyers need to demonstrate in order to get promoted to the partnership.

So get networking. Because, at the end of the day, getting promoted is not a passive thing – you don't get promoted, you promote yourself.

2 Do you want to earn more money?

When the pay rises get handed out, how do you think the organization decides who gets the most money? One might hope that the HR department would take an impartial view based on the performance of individuals to come to some rational decision. But, let's get real. In organizational life, is there any such thing as an "objective view?"

More often than not, pay rises are based on appraisals or other subjective evaluations of you. And guess what? Yes, it's the people who get themselves noticed who get the biggest pay rises.

3 Would you like to get offered a new job?

Whether you are a college leaver looking for a first job or a senior manager looking for one last job, networking can give you access to a huge market of jobs. Many jobs are not advertised – they are filled by word of mouth. And networking is nothing more than spreading your message from person to person, by word of mouth.

Even if you are not actively looking for a job, networking can create unexpected opportunities by raising your profile with headhunters. Being headhunted carries more than a little prestige with it – and with that prestige usually comes a fresh challenge, a new organization willing to pay attention to your views and experience, a bigger pay package, and maybe even a corner office with a view.

To be headhunted doesn't mean that you necessarily need to attract the attention of an executive search firm that does it for a living – although it helps. Many jobs are presented much less formally than that. Three examples: I was once offered a job after a managing director saw me speaking at a conference. I know a merchandising manager who was offered a new job when a colleague of hers moved to a new organization and recommended her. And an HR manager got an offer to transfer from Germany to the UK after making a new contact on an open training course.

If there are any new jobs to be had, networking will help you find them – by establishing contact with new people, building relationships, and making yourself memorable.

4 Do you work for yourself as a freelancer or consultant?

No matter what field you work in, networking is essential. Whether you are a full-time IT consult.ant or a part-time graphic designer, a self-employed writer or a traveling financial advisor, the key to finding people who will buy your services or products is networking.

Big businesses can afford to find clients or customers by advertising, but for the freelancer without a million-pound budget, you need to rely on word-of-mouth. And how do you get people to say good things about you? It's down to talking to as many people as you can and spreading consistent messages about you and what you do – that is, networking.

5 Are you a part of an organization that wants to succeed?

All organizations have goals. And if you want to help your organization to succeed, then networking can play a major part.

You might be the owner/partner/director of a business with a financial stake in seeing it succeed. Or perhaps you are a committed team player who believes that the goals of your organization are worthwhile. Maybe you work for a charity that needs people to volunteer their time or donate money to help your organization succeed.

Whatever you do, you need to find people who share your goals – customers or clients, or perhaps investors, volunteers, or contributors.

It's a big mistake – a huge mistake, in fact – to believe that good products or services sell themselves. Not so long ago, I used to work for a small management consulting firm that had a fantastic offering that none of our competitors were able to match. But the business lost money like a leaky bucket because no one believed that this little consulting firm could really deliver what it said it could.

And so the path to financial success is littered with tales of woe, of entrepreneurs who developed great products but couldn't find anyone to pay for them. Customers don't buy because you tell them your product is good – they buy because they trust you when you tell them it's a good product. And given that we are all bombarded on a daily basis by advertising messages, how do we know who to trust? Most of us are more likely to trust someone or something if it has been recommended to us by someone we already know – that is, one of the people in our network.

Even if you work for a large business with an enviable brand, there's got to be a reason for someone to come to you rather than one of your competitors. As an example, take the "Big Four" accountancy firms – the top handful that is able to charge a huge premium for work with the FTSE 100 and Fortune 500. Why does someone go to a partner at KPMG or Ernst & Young when PricewaterhouseCoopers is the biggest firm in the world? Rarely does a client choose one firm over another because of something he or she has read in a marketing pamphlet. More often than not, it comes down to the fact that a client has a person.al relationship with a partner at a particular firm.

Who wouldn't rather work with someone they know and trust? When partners and account managers move firms, they often take their client relationships with them – because at the end of the day, the clients are buying relationships with individuals, not the firm.

The same goes for community groups and charities. There are tens of thousands of registered charities in the United Kingdom alone. If you are trying to generate support – enlisting volunteers or raising funds – why should someone pay attention to you rather than some other cause? More often than not, it comes down to personal relationships.

Trust and relationships are common themes in networking. And while we often think of network.ing as a process of getting out there and spreading your message to as many people as you can, the same skills can also be used to focus on fewer key individuals, getting them to know you and trust you until they eventually decide to work with you.

6 Have you aspirations of working for yourself in the future?

Ever imagine being your own boss? Ever think about the luxury of being able to choose when you work, what you do, and how you do it? Whether it's next year or in ten years' time, can you foresee a time when you might want to work for yourself? Well, for literally millions of people, it's not a dream but a reality.

UK government statistics published in August 2004 said that there were 4.0 million small businesses in the United Kingdom in 2003. Of this number, 2.9 million are known to have no employees – in other words they are made up of people working for themselves. What I found interesting though, was that the number of small businesses had increased from 3.8 million in the previous year. Now, I know there are lies, damned lies, and statistics. But assuming that the figures are even reason.ably robust, that means that at least 200,000 people decided to start up their own businesses in the last year alone. And the real number could be many more than that if you assume that some businesses were set up by two or three ex-colleagues or friends getting together to become partners in a business, but still not taking on employees. Could you see yourself joining that select group of people in the near future?

Deciding to set up my own business was the best decision I have made in my career. But it would be foolish to jump ship and hurl yourself into the maelstrom of working for yourself, without knowing that you will be able to make money from it. Who will pay you to do work for them? Who will buy your products or services? If you need to raise capital to kick-start your business, who will provide the funds? Whether you are looking for clients and customers or investors, networking could be the key. So start now and build your network of contacts, so that when you are ready to make the move, you'll have all the people around you in place.

01

Get Ready to Network

It's not what you know, it's who you know

When I remind people of this age-old adage, their first response is often, "But I don't know anybody important!" But the whole point of networking is that you don't need to know anybody. One of the benefits of living in the twenty-first century is that you don't need to have a certain background to be accepted into most circles. You don't need to have been to a certain school or to have studied at a particular university. It's true that those associations still often do help – but the good news is that they are no longer essential. Most managers and decision makers are happy to be approached by anybody – as long as that "anybody" has something of value to contribute.

But I still haven't answered the criticism that you may not "know anybody important." There's a popular concept called "six degrees of separation," which argues that everyone on the planet is connected to every other person on the planet through a chain of contacts that has no more than five links. So by getting in touch with someone who knows someone who knows someone who knows someone who knows someone, you should be able to find your way to anyone.

Clear as mud?

Let's take things back to a simpler time, the 1960s. An American social psychologist, Stanley Milgram, was particularly interested in social networks and a big believer that the world really is a small place. He tested the theory by asking people in Omaha (it's in the mid-West, I'm reliably informed) to send packages to a complete stranger on the east coast of the United States. The senders were told only the stranger's name and occupation and that the stranger lived somewhere in Massachusetts. And they were instructed that in order to locate the stranger, they had to send the package to a person they knew on a first-name basis who they thought might be able to pass it on to someone who might personally know the mysterious stranger.

Although many of the senders expected the chain to include dozens and dozens of people, it transpired that it took on average only between five and seven links to get most of the packages delivered.

More recently, when scientists tried to replicate the experiment in 2003, with more than 60,000 people in 166 different countries, they found pretty much the same thing too. Most people are separated by only six degrees.

So whoever you're looking for – perhaps a business angel offering to invest in your start-up business, a career mentor, or customers or volunteers to work on a community project – you can always meet someone new who may know some.

one who could introduce you to the very people you are looking for.

Networking ain't rocket science

The good news is that networking is a learnable skill. It's not something innate that you either have or you haven't got.

When I was a teenager, I was so shy that I sometimes used to hide in the toilets or the locker room rather than go talk to my classmates. Rather than give talks to my class of only a dozen other school children, I would lie and say that I had appointments with doctors or dentists. But over the years, I have conquered my fear of meeting strangers. I even enjoy standing up in front of large groups and giving formal presentations. Nowadays, most people assume that I'm an extravert. But I'm not – I'm simply an introvert who has learnt how to network effectively.

You might think that being an extravert helps – but your level of introversion or extraversion has little to do with effective networking. It's true that extraverts are happier to talk to strangers – but many extraverts talk too much and about the wrong sorts of topics. Introverts, on the other hand, may feel more uncomfortable approaching strangers, but on the plus side tend to be better listeners. So you can be a good networker irrespective of whether you are naturally extraverted or introverted.

But what is networking exactly?

It is simply a technique for presenting yourself effectively when you meet people so that they will want to meet and deal with you again. When I talk about meeting "people," these could be entirely new contacts that you are meeting for the first time, or colleagues and acquaintances that you have known for some time.

And when you have built a sufficient degree of trust with them, you can move on to discussing whether there are opportunities for you to help each other. These opportunities could take the form of sharing information with each other, or making introductions to further, new contacts.

Let's be honest about this, though. I'm not suggesting that you look to help people out of the goodness of your heart. It's all about reciprocity.

If you scratch their back, they'll scratch yours.

What goes around, comes around.

Looking for ways to help them out is ultimately a means to an end. You are banking favors so that they will eventually feel that they need to help you out too.

When you have built the relationship and helped your contacts, then you can try to access the people in their networks too. Because the whole point of networking – and we're back to the six degrees of separation argument here – is that you don't need to know anyone important. Instead, someone in your network may know someone in their network who is "important."

To sum up then, networking requires that you talk to people, listen to what they have to say, and present yourself well to them. Does that sound so sinister or difficult?

Setting an objective

Many people network strategically – they have a goal in mind while they meet people. So which of the six scenarios above did you most relate to?

I am not saying that one of them should mirror your circumstances exactly. In fact, having too specific a goal when networking is a bad idea because it may close you off to other opportunities. But perhaps you might feel slightly more empathy with one than another.

For me, as a partner in a small business, I'm usually prowling for opportunities to find clients. A marketing manager who I'm coaching at the moment is on the lookout for a new job that will allow him to leave the financial services industry to work in a sector with more physically tangible products such as consumer goods or the automotive industry.

It's worth taking a few minutes to think about your objectives. Because it is actually quite difficult to network *effectively* if you don't know what you want to get out of it. Of course you can still meet and greet people, but having a particular objective should color everything you say and do. It should affect how you talk about yourself and alter the tactics you employ for making contact and staying in touch.

So please do it now. Have a think. Yes, really. Don't just read on, thinking that you'll do it later – because the rest of this book will be so much more useful if you have an objective to underpin the rest of your reading. Put the book down for a moment and have a think about it.

If you are struggling, another way of looking at it is to ask yourself where you would like to be in three to five years' time. The smug reply I usually get back is "On a beach, having won the lottery." But there's a difference between having a dream and a fantasy. Winning millions on the lottery isn't very likely to happen – perhaps it's more of a fantasy than a dream (statisticians always tell us that we are more likely to get struck by lightning or stung to death by a bee than win the lottery). But wanting to be promoted to director level within four years or running your own business in three years, that's a dream that feels more realistic.

I can't urge you enough to come up with an objective.

Once you have one, keep your objective in mind. Is it worth writing down on a scrap of paper or in the margin of this book?

If not strategic, then spontaneous is okay too

Ninety percent of people network strategically with a specific objective in mind, but some of us may honestly not be seeking anything in particular at the moment. But you can still be open to spontaneous approaches and want to make a good impression on other people. Because *you never know* when your career might take a new direction.

You might love your job today, but an ex-colleague could suddenly ring you and ask if you would like to set up a business with him or her. And do you know anyone who might be willing to invest?

You might find yourself the hapless victim of a mass redundancy program next week and need to find a job. Or your husband/wife, boyfriend/girlfriend might get offered a promotion 200 miles away. How would you start your job search if you wanted to go with them?

So while it is okay to not want to get anything out of networking, it is still worth thinking about how you introduce yourself to people and keep track of the people that you meet. Because you never know.

Network anywhere

An ex-boss of mine managed to get a major client by networking through his nanny. John and his wife used to have a "nanny share" with another couple that had a young child of a similar age. John got to know the other couple and over the course of months managed to share enough information with them that they recommended that he get in touch with another friend of theirs, who eventually turned into a six-figure client.

Many novices assume networking is a process that is limited mainly to conferences or trade shows – events that they might attend only a couple of times a year. But the skill of networking can be adapted to just about any situation in which you are meeting new people. Think about when you are sent on training courses by your employer. Or when you are asked to join a new project team as part of a cross-departmental initiative. How about when you go to a meeting with a new client? Just because you may not win work from a client there and then does not mean that you cannot keep in touch, develop a relationship with the client, and find other ways to help each other out.

Even meeting suppliers could be an opportunity. I once got a new client when I invited three website designers to pitch for a project to completely revamp my corporate website. I kept in touch with the two web designers who didn't get the work and offered both of them feedback on why they did not win the work. When I arranged to have a coffee with one of them, it turned out that he had lost a number of pitches in recent months – and he agreed to pay me to coach him on his pitching and presentation skills.

Then there are the social situations. You might meet new friends at a mutual friend's birthday or leaving drinks. What about celebrations such as anniversary parties or weddings? Or how about meeting other parents at your child's parent– teacher evening?

If you are serious about networking, you will find that there are actually very few places where you can't network.

What do you do?

"I'm an accountant." "I'm an IT systems support manager." "I'm an HR business partner." It might be technically correct to use your job title. But is that how you want to be remembered? Does it sum up all the aspects of what you do and what you enjoy doing, capture your experience, and hint at your objective?

Probably not.

When you meet someone for the first time, business etiquette dictates that you say "hello" and exchange names.

No surprises so far. But after this initial pleasantry, the commonest question someone will ask you is, "What do you do?"

Think about a new way to describe yourself – I call it my "blurb" – one that tells the other person a bit more about you. Because the aim is to give them conversational hooks that will allow them to ask you further questions about what you do.

It has to capture their attention too. Julian Goldsmith, managing director of public relations agency ARC Business, describes his work by saying, "I undertake the writing of press releases, articles, speeches, and reports. I arrange journalist interviews, organize events, and place people in conference speaking slots." Not terribly exciting, is it? But he realizes that and so redeems himself by always starting off by saying: "I make business people famous." Wow – what a great hook. Who wouldn't want to hear more?

Good words to include in your blurb include "support," "help," "teach," "provide," "eliminate," "maintain," and "improve" – verbs that will immediately help the other person to understand what you have to offer.

Or what about "solve," "speed up," "decrease," "grow," "strengthen," or "relieve"?

Saying that you are "an accountant" could mean almost anything. Is there anything more interesting that you would like to get across? Perhaps you want to emphasize your experience to potential employers by saying that you work as "an accountant in the finance function of a large business, so I help them with strategic planning and capital investment decisions." If you are looking for customers of a certain size, then maybe you are "an accountant specializing in providing bookkeeping and tax planning services for small businesses" or "an accountant in audit working primarily with national and international clients." Or the hook might be to say (with a touch of irony), "I make people richer."

Instead of "an IT systems support manager," how about, "I solve technical problems for a group of 100 people, whether they are in the office or working from a client's location."

Rather than saying you are "an HR business partner," perhaps you could say, "I'm an HR business partner, helping line managers with the strategic side of managing people through recruitment and training."

What you say in your blurb depends on the circumstances too. And it is worth preparing variations on your basic theme. The above descriptions might be appropriate for approaching someone at a conference. But when you are introducing your.self at the start of a two-day training workshop, you would be justified in taking a few more sentences.

For example, the HR business partner might say:

I'm an HR business partner working at Imperial Biotech, a specialist pharmaceutical company. I support a business unit of 250 people on the more strategic people issues that they face, which typically means recruitment and development. While an operational HR manager looks after recruitment of junior staff, I support the directors in recruiting and selecting senior managers. And I provide one-to-one coaching for the directors and senior managers.

Introducing yourself at an ex-colleague's birthday drinks in such a stiff and formal way would raise eyebrows. And doing it at your child's parent–teacher evening at school will almost certainly get you shunned. So have different blurbs for different spheres of your life. But in every case, think five to ten seconds. And that's ten seconds max.

Finally, after you have told the other person(s) what you do, you must return the favor. In a one-on-one situation, it would be by asking, "And what do you do?" In a group, it might simply be by making eye contact with and gesturing to the person next to you.

Develop an elevator speech

The lift doors open on the first floor and you get in to come face-to-face with Richard Branson, Donald Trump, someone big and impressive, a mover and shaker. He sees you gawping at him and says, "Yes? You have until I get off on the 12th floor for you to give me your pitch. So what do you have to say for yourself?"

It is a bit of a fantasy scenario admittedly. But it has given rise to the elevator speech. In most networking situations, it isn't appropriate to give too lengthy a reply to the question, "What do you do?" After all, the question is said as much out of politeness as it is in a genuine interest to find out about you.

On rare occasions, however, someone will be upfront and ask you what you're looking for. Need an investor? Selling a product or service? Or selling the product that is you? It's a very direct – very North American – approach (hence "elevator" rather than "lift"), often employed by people who cannot be bothered with the more social side of networking. And having someone be so direct can completely fluster would-be networkers. So have a 20 to 30-second blurb ready – your elevator speech.

For instance, a market researcher might say:

> I'm an account director at Donovan Ashford, a leading marketing research consultancy. We look after clients who need greater insight about their customers. We offer both qualitative and quantitative research methods through our network of eighteen offices worldwide to provide a seamless service to international clients. If I could take your card, I'd be delighted to set up a meeting and give you the opportunity to see why world-leading companies such as Coca Cola and Sony come to us to understand their customers.

One hundred words. That's all it needs.

An unemployed operations manager looking for a new job might say:

> I was until recently operations manager for an airline. But after seven years, I was made redundant due to a downturn in the industry. So I am now looking to transfer my skills into an operations role in other sectors. I'm looking to meet people who might be able to help me in my search – perhaps by giving me advice about the job market or by putting me in touch with recruiters. Do you think you might know anyone who might be willing to speak to me on the telephone for 15 minutes?

Or a self-employed electrician looking to offer his services might say:

> I'm an electrical engineer working in the Greater Manchester area. I'm qualified, certified, and insured to carry out wiring and rewiring work, including outdoor and indoor lighting, and mounting devices such as sockets, switches, doorbells, and CCTV cameras. I work with homes and business.es, and no job is too big or small. I think you'll find me reliable and cost-effective, so I would like to offer you my card in case you ever have the need for an electrical engineer.

Networking clubs are growing in popularity amongst freelance workers and small business owners and are another opportunity to deliver an extended elevator speech. At such events, some of the time is typically devoted to informal network.ing, in which you are expected to ask and respond to questions as at any other event. But at some point, the group will typically gather together and everyone is asked to give a longer – perhaps two or three minutes – speech about themselves.

It is a good idea to have an elevator speech ready in case anyone asks you for yours. However, I would never advocate that you ask anyone you are meeting for the first time for theirs, as they may think that your directness borders on rudeness.

Once more with feeling

When it comes to elevator speeches, three minutes can feel like a long, long time if you are not word perfect.

It is worth writing out what you would say. More importantly though, practice speaking it out loud. Too often, people write the speech out but do not rehearse delivering it – and that is a big mistake to make. Even if you can memorize all of the words (which is a big assumption), are you delivering it in an enthusiastic, exciting manner?

Many of the people that I coach on networking are happy to write it out – but when I ask them to tell their elevator speech to me, they deliver it in a flat and lifeless manner.

Rehearse your elevator speech and, ideally, record the sound of your voice. How does it sound? Once you get over the unfamiliarity of hearing your voice as others hear you, concentrate on delivering it in a passionate manner. Think about when you take breaths. Pauses are often used to convey drama. Think about how to transmit emotion. Would it help to raise the tone of your voice or to lower it?

Once you have done that, amend it and practice it even more. Put it away for a few days then listen to yourself speaking it out loud. Tweak and practice it again and again to ensure that you can get your message across without hesitating, fumbling over words, or repeating yourself.

Understand the product

An advert from the personals column of a national newspaper claims:

> Issue-free single guy, handsome and attractive,
> no beer gut, late 30s. Independent, caring and
> loving, GSOH, genuine and reliable. Looking
> for a woman who I can spark with.

(By the way, GSOH is personals-speak for "good sense of humor.") Assuming that he's not lying outright about anything, should we take him for his word that he is all – or even any – of these things?

The problem is that many people just do not see themselves in the same way that others see them. He might think he is "handsome and attractive" while strangers might describe him as plain or even a bit odd looking. Or his definition of "reliable" may be that he is never more than 45 minutes late when meeting dates.

And so it is the same with networking. You might think you are confident, but others might think you are quite shy. Or, worse, they may think you are too confident – bordering on arrogant.

If you think you are trusting, others may perceive you as gullible. Honesty could be seen by others as tactlessness; spontaneity seen as disorganization.

To help you create the right impression when networking, a great exercise is to get some feed.back on your strengths and weaknesses. I'd recommend sending out a simple questionnaire to a handful of colleagues and ex-colleagues, acquaintances, and other people who know you well at work. Avoid family or close friends, as they may not be able to give you as objective a picture as you need.

The questionnaire need not be complicated. What is more important is to ensure that responses are anonymous – to encourage people to respond – and that you act on the feedback you receive.

As few as three questions could do the job:

1. What do you think my strengths are?
2. What do you think my weaknesses are?
3. What advice would you give me in order to help me to be more effective in my working relationships?

Add an introductory letter to explain why you are doing this. Personalize each letter to flatter the respondent. But emphasize why it is important, for example: "I am trying to gather other people's perspectives on how I come across to them. This is an important part of my career development and I would be most grateful if you could answer the following three questions."

Then send out the questionnaires along with a stamped, self-addressed envelope. Yes, I am telling you to use snail mail. In our age of email, we are inundated by electronic missives trying to catch our attention – emails from colleagues that have nothing to do with us, forwarded jokes, and invitations to buy everything from mortgages to sex toys. Your request for help could easily get lost in such a barrage of email. But when was the last time you received a note addressed personally to you with a stamp on it and a handwritten covering letter?

Look the part

In the hit television series *Sex and the City*, Sarah Jessica Parker's character, Carrie Bradshaw, had a dazzling array of outfits and hundreds of pairs of shoes. Personally, I think that she dressed more like a call girl than a fashion icon, but then I'm what creative and fashion types would call a "suit."

A dark suit means business in the legal and financial circles. But low-slung designer jeans and a couple of inches of exposed midriff are de rigueur for TV producers – and that's just the men.

First impressions count. Whenever two people meet, they each make snap judgments about each other based only on first impressions. These judgments may not be accurate or fair, but that does not stop us from making them. The very first impression you make happens long before you open your mouth to speak. Dress the wrong way, and your networking opportunities may shun you more quickly than if you had smeared yourself in dog poo.

In affluent west London, I know a 50-something managing director of a property business and her two female senior managers who all wear a corporate uniform of blue jeans, white fitted top, and navy jacket. To finish it off, they all wear perilously high heels. But it works for them – their business has a funky culture and they deal with clients who appreciate that you can look smart without having to wear a suit.

What to wear or not to wear is a book in itself. But no book would ever be able to tell you exactly what is right for any given situation, as sectors vary from each other in too many subtle ways.

It is human nature to like people who are like us. When we meet someone who was at the same university, grew up in the same town, or shares a sporting interest with us, we instantly find him or her more interesting. And the same thing happens on a subconscious level with our clothes. We are far more likely to approach – or allow ourselves to be approached by – people who have a similar look to ourselves.

What does your look say about you? I'm not going to tell you what you should be wearing. But most of us should probably invest more time and effort in our clothes if we are to create perfect first impressions. Because it really can help to make other people feel comfortable with us and want to talk to us.

And smell your parts

I promised at the start of the book not to treat you like a dummy or an idiot. But I am going to wave a nagging finger at you for just a few moments. Because it always amazes me that personal hygiene is an issue for a greater proportion of highly educated and otherwise bright people than you would expect.

Let's try a test. Lick the back of your hand. Stick your tongue out all the way and give the back of your hand a big fat lick, like you're a slobbering dog. Go on, you can do it. Try it now. If you're reading this on a train or a plane, just make sure that no one sees you, as they will think you are deranged.

Now wave your hand in the air and count to ten to let it dry. You'll feel the back of your hand cooling as it dries. Now sniff it. How does it smell? Maybe of the coffee you had an hour ago? Maybe there is a hint of garlic from that delicious Italian you had at lunch? Or, if you are a bit dehydrated, it could be a bit rancid. Ugh.

Would you want the smell of someone's breakfast pumped in your direction during a conversation? No? So don't do it to others. Keep in mind that the smell of your breath is detectable over two feet away. And two to three feet is about the distance that most people stand apart from each other when they meet for the first time, shake hands, and detect any unpleasant odors.

You can have a great elevator speech, but no one will want to hear it if their nose is screaming, "Get me out of here!" Breath mints and chewing gum – buy some now. They immediately mask stale odors. And sucking on something or chewing something releases saliva, which is your body's natural mouthwash and defense against their return. Some people argue that business cards are a would-be networker's most critical accessory – but I'd argue that you won't be able to get anyone to take your card if no one is willing to talk to you because of your bad breath.

Body odor is another big problem for a surprising number of people. And it is a big problem because you can't smell your own body odor. We are all immune to our own true smell.

The reason is something called "habituation." Psychologists have discovered that our brain uses habituation to allow us to turn off stimuli that are no longer interesting. For example, when you first sit down during a meeting, you notice the sensation of the chair against your buttocks. But after a while, you forget about the sensation of the chair because you focus on what's being said and what you need to say. Your brain habituates – or gets used to the feel of the chair – and decides to deprioritize it.

And it is exactly the same for your brain and how you smell. The smell receptors in your nose probably did tell your brain that you smelt a bit funny – but that happened way, way back in puberty. But after a few days, your brain decided to stop bothering to make you aware that you reek.

I'm not saying that you do for certain stink. But I am saying that the only way to know if you need to get a more powerful deodorant (or to apply it more than once or twice during the day) is to ask a close friend. And be aware that body odor does intensify throughout the day. I recently presented at a conference and noticed that my fellow presenter – who sat next to me for the whole day – became more "fragrant" as the day progressed.

Okay, now that you look (and smell) great, let's move on to what you say.

02

Build your Network, One Person at a Time

It's okay to feel nervous, but JFDI

Million-selling author Susan Jeffers has probably made a fortune out of a book aimed at helping people deal with unhappy personal relationships and confront difficult situations. And while discussing the content would take us off on a tangent, it's the title that I like – *Feel the Fear and Do It Anyway*.

When we are growing up, we are taught not to talk to strangers. But when we network, the whole point is to approach as many strangers as possible. So it is perfectly natural that we should feel apprehensive or even downright terrified to go talk to new people when everything about our upbringing is telling us not to.

I have been networking for many years now, and still feel my heart pounding when I enter a room crowded with people. Everyone seems to be clustered in small groups apart from me. They all seem to be discussing matters of national – no, international – importance, and who am I to dare to interrupt them?

When I have to speak at a workshop or conference, I sometimes wake up at around five in the morning, mind roiling and worrying about things that could go wrong. And it doesn't get better when I approach the lectern. Sometimes the nerves are so acute that I can feel myself wanting to throw up – but I cover it up by coughing and pretending that I am clearing my throat.

But, to paraphrase Susan Jeffers, you feel the fear but – because you are a person who has goals and aspirations that you want to achieve – decide to get on with it anyway.

Here are a few techniques that will help you to overcome the nerves.

How do you eat an elephant? One bite at a time. The first technique, then, is to set a manageable bite-sized objective for any networking event. Often, it is the size of a task that can send us running. Thinking that you are going to "network" is simply too unwieldy and immeasurable a task, so your brain can't process the scale of what it needs to do. But deciding that you are going to approach three people on their own and engage them in conversation before heading off for a coffee and a muffin to congratulate yourself is entirely manageable. In fact, if you think about it, three people is nothing! Bah, you could probably speak to half a dozen before you go get that coffee.

How about deciding that you are going to exchange business cards with at least two people in a room? Or that you will stand by the self-serve coffee table and ask four people if you can get them a drink as an ice breaker? Keep your bite-sized objective small and achievable. You can always set yourself a bigger task when you have realized the first.

The second technique is to calm yourself by overcoming the physical symptoms of tension. When we are nervous, we take shallow breaths into the top of our lungs. Our chest rises and falls when we pant in a nervous fashion. But when we are relaxed, we use something called "diaphragmatic breathing" – we breathe slowly and deeply into the lower part of our lungs, and our bellies rise and fall instead.

The great thing about the body and brain is that they are inextricably linked. Stress and tension can cause our bodies to react negatively. But we can also calm our brains down by forcing our bodies to adopt relaxed breathing.

Practice your breathing by lying on a bed or sofa. Put your right hand on your chest and your left hand on your stomach. Now inhale and exhale, taking fast, short breaths into your lungs, concentrating on expanding only your chest area. Your right hand should be rising and falling while your left hand stays static. When you do this 20 or 30 times, you will feel dizzy. Shallow breathing makes you feel nervous.

Now try diaphragmatic breathing by taking long, slow breaths into your belly. Your left hand should rise and fall, while your right hand stays completely still. Count to four as you inhale and another four as you exhale. Once you get it right, it will send you into an almost trance-like state and your fingers and toes may tingle as your body relaxes and sends blood to your extremities.

When you have practiced the technique enough times, you will be able to snap into diaphragmatic breathing – and generate a feeling of calm – whenever you need it.

So, feel the fear and do it anyway. Or, to borrow from the strap line of the world's largest branded sportswear company (but at the same time, with apologies to their legal team), my personal motto is: "It's okay to feel nervous, but just f***ing do it."

Recite a personal mantra

CBT is an acronym with multiple meanings. If you happen to be a sadomasochist, it can mean something physically quite painful (I'll give you a clue – the "T" stands for torture). But to psychologists, it stands for "cognitive behavioral therapy."

A central plank of CBT – the psychological kind – is that cognitions (psychospeak for "thoughts" – why don't they simply call them thoughts??) can affect behavior, and behavior can affect cognitions.

Therapists use this link to treat clinical depression. Forcing people to behave in a particular way can affect how they think and feel. To be more precise, forcing patients to perform happy behavior – even when they feel incredibly depressed – can turn negative cognitions into positive ones, helping to lift their mood.

Do something enough times, and you will eventually feel it too. If you think relaxed and confident thoughts, you will banish nerves when you are preparing to network. And that's where the personal mantra comes in.

Scripting and repeating a sequence of positive phrases is guaranteed to dispel the blackest of moods. But you must articulate the words clearly and say them with conviction, preferably out loud.

What works for you may not work for some.one else. But personally, I fix my face into a big smile and repeat to myself: "I am successful. I am confident. I can speak to anyone I want to here. Smile, smile, smile."

It's cheesy and sounds ridiculous. But trust me, I'm a psychologist. It works – JFDI. Just be care.ful not to do it within earshot of anyone unless you want them to think you are communing with voices from the spirit world.

Make the first move

I saw a poster on a train recently. I forget what the product was, but it related a parable of a lonely man who was so poor that he often went hungry. He had nothing to eat, and his only possession was a tall painter's ladder. But he lived next door to another lonely, hungry man. And, guess what? This second man's only possession was a tall apple tree. But because neither of them was brave enough to talk to each other, both remained hungry.

Okay, it's a corny story, but aren't all parables? You're a bright person and you get the point.

Unless you go talk to people, you will never know if someone wants – or even desperately and urgently needs and is willing to pay a premium for – your particular ladder.

You might argue that at a conference of, for example, IT professionals there could be hundreds of people with ladders to offer – and not many people milling around with tall apple trees. But, to extend the parable, perhaps the apples are 12 feet off the ground and other people's ladders are too short or too long, while your ladder happens to be 12 feet long. Or perhaps the lower branches are densely packed and other people's ladders are too wide to penetrate the lower branches to reach the plump and juicy apples.

Even when there are two of you with identical ladders – who would they rather work with? Of course it is the person they like more.

You would be surprised how many people are terrified of networking events, so it's up to you to make the first move.

Look for anyone standing on their own. Breaking into groups is more difficult, so try to approach individuals to begin with. People standing near stands or serving themselves at a drinks table are also a good bet.

Avoid people who are moving. They may be going somewhere – perhaps to meet someone, engage someone else in conversation, or because they urgently need to find a toilet. Wait until they are stationary.

And the first move is actually five flowing sequential moves that should blend almost seamlessly into one. Smile, eye contact, approach, handshake, and speak:

1. When you spot someone that you would like to approach, compose yourself and smile. Babies from the age of several weeks are able to recognize smiles and so we are pre-programmed to respond positively to smiles.

2. Keep smiling until you make eye contact. Then "flash" your eyes – lift your eyebrows slightly to show the other person that you recognize the fact that you have made eye contact.

3. If the other person maintains eye contact – which can be for as little as two seconds, such is the power of eye contact – then approach them. As you get within several feet of them, begin to raise your right hand in readiness of a handshake.

4. Give them a firm handshake. By firm, ensure that you open up your thumb and first finger to allow the webbed area between to touch their webbed area. But there is no need to grip too hard – this isn't a test of physical strength.

5. Speak.

But what do you say?

Most people start with an introduction along the lines of: "I'm Rob. I thought I would say hello" or "I'm Rob. I hope you don't mind, but I thought I would introduce myself."

The key is then to ask a question that gets the other person talking. Start with one neutral question or statement about your shared circumstances, such as:

• "What brings you to this conference/seminar/ etcetera?"

• "How do you know the host/company/ etcetera?"

• "It's much busier here than I would have expected. How are you finding it here today?"

Continue with other neutral questions that encourage the other person to reveal more about themselves. But make sure that you ask open questions – ones that cannot be answered with a simple "yes" or "no":

- "How did you hear about this event?"
- "How are you finding it compared with other events you have been to?"
- "How was your journey here?"
- "And what do you do?"

That's all there is to making the first move.

More icebreakers

"We all need to shit, shower, and shave." I could-n't track down who originally came up with the phrase, but it's true that whether you are a junior apprentice or a chief executive we all have these things in common.

And that's the only purpose of the first few minutes of conversation – establishing common ground. Some people deride it as small talk or chitchat, but custom dictates that we need small talk to build up to the big stuff. It is simply too early to talk about your objective (unless you are asked directly for your elevator speech – see above). People hate feeling used, and sharing your objective with someone – or even hinting at it – will be an instant turn off at this point. Even if you really are networking only to use people to help you fulfill your objective, you need to be subtler than that.

Small talk builds rapport and is an essential prerequisite to doing business. But just a few minutes' planning before any event will arm you with plenty of topics for rapport-building conversation.

Skim through the newspapers that morning and look for relevant stories. If you are going to a business event, then focus on the business section. If it is a non-business event, look for general topics of conversation. But stay away from controversial topics such as political/religious discussions that could alienate others.

Another tip is to find three things to say about the event you are at. Make a statement, but then use it to ask a question of the other person. For example:

- "Have you been to the Glaxotech stand yet? They have a really interesting display illustrating their R&D process. Have you seen it yet?"
- "Did you go to the talk by Bill Bates? He had a couple of really interesting points to make about the IT industry. He said that…. What do you think?"
- "I met Jennifer, our host, at her colleague's leaving drinks. How do you know her?"

Common gripes are another way to keep the conversation going. Everyone hates bad weather. Everyone hates being stuck in traffic. Everyone worries about the quality of the food at faceless convention centers. But be careful not to spend too long being negative. One shared complaint is a talking point, but two or three will make you sound off-putting.

Don't worry that you should be talking busi.ness. In the first few minutes of conversation, the aim is to appear relaxed and to project the impression that you are an interesting person. Just about any topics of conversation would do – such as sports you play or follow, or think more broadly about the world of media and entertainment. Is there a big hit television show that everyone is talking about? What about a film that you saw recently? Or a book that you read?

But don't lie. If you pretend to have read a weighty management tome when you haven't, it is just inviting someone to catch you out on it. So it is a good idea to plan ahead to allow you to appear spontaneous. People used to ask me and my mind would go blank. Or the only thing that I remembered reading was one of the *Harry Potter* books, which might have made the wrong impression. So think ahead of a film or book that will create the right impression. And then be ready to describe it in two or three sentences.

Classic conversation killers

Can I put forward a motion to ban the word "fine" from the English language?

Whether you are meeting someone for the first time or seeing them again, it's polite to ask, "How are you?" And in our busy world, the natural response is to respond automatically with "Fine," or "Great, thanks."

That may be acceptable when you are greeting a colleague in the lift at work or running past an acquaintance when you are late for a train. But in the context of networking, it is a classic conversa.tion killer. Because you have answered an open question with a closed response.

The same goes for "What have you been up to?" and "What's up?"

The polite response is, again, along the lines of "Nothing much." or "Same old, same old." But there you go again, killing the conversation.

Instead, your answer is an ideal opportunity to start hinting about – or at least moving the conversation in the general direction of – your ultimate objective. If you are looking for a new job, then perhaps now is the time to nudge the conversation in the direction of the skills you have. If you are trying to recruit someone, then maybe it is appropriate to talk in exasperation about the problems that your team is facing without that key person.

In response to "How are you?" perhaps you could say:

- "Great thanks. I left Armstrong, Ball, & Harrison a few months ago to set up my own business." (This speaker is inviting the other person to ask: "And what is your business?" in the lead-up to his objective of looking for more clients.)
- "Incredibly busy at the moment. I've just taken on the portfolio for United Products to add to everything else I do." (This person's objective is to find a new job, and he is trying to showcase his experience of managing corporate customers.)
- "I'm really excited because I just had a positive phone call with a potential investor, so we've now got over 50 percent of the capital we need for our venture." (This person is leading up to asking for other people who might be interested in her business start-up.)

Or in response to "what have you been up to?"

- "I just had a great meeting with …"
- "I've been in the office late every night because …"
- "I've been gearing up for the launch of our new product …"

Conversation is supposed to be spontaneous, and most of us can be interesting and interested for a few minutes. But there's a key difference between socializing and networking. Chatting in a directionless manner may make 10 or 20 minutes pass pleasantly – that's socializing. But if you want to learn about others, connect and network effectively, it helps to plan ahead to allow you to guide people toward your objective in a subtle and seemingly spontaneous manner.

Are you still awake?

I don't know about you, but I have mastered the art of transporting my mind elsewhere when I'm listening to a boring speaker, lecturer, workshop facilitator, client, colleague, and so on. The only problem comes when someone asks for my input, "And what do you think about that, Rob?" Oops. What is the "that" they are talking about!?

When you network, it's almost a given that you need to listen to what is being said. After all, the other person might mention the name of someone you should get in touch with, or might give you license to get in touch. And if you miss gems like that, you may as well not bother.

But while most of us are pretty good at listening, not all of us are so naturally gifted when it comes to *appearing* as if we are listening. Think back to colleagues or acquaintances you know, who have stony, impassive faces. They are unreadable, impenetrable, and hard work to talk to.

Think about it. Listening is essentially a passive activity – if that isn't an oxymoron. You don't have to exert physical effort or strain any muscles – your ears just, well, hear. In theory, you could close your eyes and still be listening.

The problem comes in the fact that the person speaking to you needs visual cues to keep him or her interested. And that's why psychologists have coined the phrase "dynamic listening." Indicating to the people around you that you are entranced by their every word involves four cues:

1 Nodding – why do we nod? We nod when we agree with what is being said. So nodding is a great way to show that you are following the gist of the conversation.
2 Flashing – poets and artists never tire of reminding us that the eyes are the windows to the soul. And "flashing" your eyes by raising your eyebrows occasionally tells someone that you understand what is being said.
3 Smiling – it helps to mirror the mood and expressions of the people speaking to you. Even if the mood is fairly neutral, it helps to give the occasional smile to encourage them.
4 Murmuring – small noises such as "Mmm" and "Uh-

huh," or words such as "Yes" and "Go on," are more vocal indications that you are listening.

Written down, these cues can easily seem artificial. After all, non-verbal cues must be wielded with great subtlety. But now that you understand the four components of dynamic listening, watch and listen to other people, and see how they put them into action. Observe, learn from them, mimic if you must.

Don't overdo it, or people will think you have a facial tick or a psychological problem. But, used in moderation, you will have people believing that you are entirely rapt – even if you are secretly wonder.ing what to have for dinner when you get home.

Move into second and third gear

Arguing the merits of *Star Wars* over *Titanic* or bonding over your mutual hate of winter morn.ings is perfectly acceptable as establishing initial commonalities go. But as the conversation pro.gresses, you will need to steer the discussion onto business topics.

There are two reasons for doing it. First, it gets your companions talking about their work, which allows you to figure out whether they are the sorts of person who might have the connections to other people that you are looking for. Second, asking them about their work will eventually allow you to talk about yours.

Slowly, inch-by-inch, we are edging towards our objective.

Good questions to ask might include a handful from the following:

- "What do you do?" or "What line of business are you in?"
- "How did you get into that line of business?"
- "Who do you work for?"
- "How long have you worked for them?"
- "And where did you work before that?"
- "What do you most enjoy about the work?"
- "What qualifications did you need to do that?"
- "Where did you study that?"
- "Where do you think your industry is going?"

Whenever possible, try to link the other person's responses to your own experience. Consider the following:

- "Didn't their offices used to be based in Birmingham? I'm sure that one of the guys in marketing used to work there before joining us. When were you there? Perhaps you know him?"
- "My nephew is thinking about studying architecture at university. What advice would you have for him?"
- "It's interesting you say that the HR function is trying to become more strategic. The HR department in our business has just restructured along similar lines, causing all sorts of problems. How smoothly did you make the transition in your organization?"

With each question and follow-up question, look for ways to take the conversation deeper. While small talk allows you to skim across many different subjects, the aim now is to find out much more about this person.

Conversation, not interrogation

"You vill tell us zee answer," says the Gestapo offi.cer in trademark uniform and knee-high patent leather jackboots in just about any Second World War movie you care to mention. Okay, you aren't shining a spotlight in anyone's face or slapping them with your leather-gloved hand while they are tied to a chair. But being on the receiving end of a barrage of unrelenting questions can make people feel like they are being cross-examined.

A conversation should be a two-way dialog. It's a dance in which both parties take it in turn to assume the lead, switching effortlessly from being questioner to responder and back again. You ask a question, the other person replies, perhaps you make a comment on their response, which in turn allows them to ask you a question, and so on. And if you don't want to be left with no one to dance with, you need to have something to say about yourself.

A rule of thumb for getting the balance right is to allow the other person to speak two-thirds of the time, and for you to speak one-third of the time.

Whenever you ask a question, be prepared for the same question to be bounced back at you. Even if the other person doesn't ask the question, you need to interject occasionally in order to keep the conversation interactive.

For example, if you had asked someone what they had studied at university and were told that they had studied French, you might add, "I was never much good with languages. I studied chem.istry at university but then I retrained as a solicitor because the prospects are so much better in this country for lawyers than scientists."

Cunningly, then, the response takes a convoluted route through university and back to your current career.

Or, if you had asked about what they most enjoy about their work: "I would find it so difficult to deal with customers all of the time. I only have to deal with internal customers, but that's challenging enough for me. I doubt I'd be any good at handling questions and complaints from customers all day. I prefer to spend my time on more strategic issues."

Think of each response as an attempt to lead the other person from A to Z. A is what they last talked about and Z is a topic related to your objective – perhaps a skill or experience or goal that you want to mention. But be prepared to travel from A to Z via D and J, K and T.

Have a tale to tell

Picture this: A filter on a vacuum cleaner breaks down, spewing a high-pressure jet of dust and carpet fluff in a cloud over the entire room that you've just cleaned. Even worse, the room you've just cleaned is the workspace of a couple of dozen investment bankers who are due to start work in less than an hour.

Bit of a nightmare scenario, right?

And that's what is so cunning about this story that someone once told me at a networking breakfast meeting – it created a picture in my mind. There were 20 or more other people at the networking event. But the person telling me the story – the managing director of an office clean.ing company – managed to stand out above the rest. By sharing this simple story with me, he created 10 times more impact than by merely telling me what he and his business did.

We meet so many people in our lives, and the names and faces blur within hours – if not minutes – of meeting them. Give it a week, and they will be entirely forgotten.

And that's the risk of simply telling other people what you do. You'll be instantly forgettable too. But stories that create an image in your mind can last for a very long time. And that is why anecdotes are your most powerful weapon for making a lasting impression.

It takes more preparation on your part, I'm afraid. Again, the idea is to create the impression that you are an interesting person – the kind of person that they would want to hear from again.

But people have short attention spans, so keep your stories short. Practice saying them out loud, and time yourself. Less than two minutes is ideal. Three minutes is bearable. And four is almost certain to incite attempts by your listener to get away from you.

Averted disasters make for good anecdotes. We live in a tabloid society that craves bad news. Pick up a newspaper or watch the news, and you'll read stories of scandal and disaster, tragedy, and ruin.

The office cleaning managing director went on to tell me how he had received a frantic phone call from the cleaning supervisor about the broken vacuum cleaner and how he had sorted it out. So the story finishes with a happy ending after all. Phew.

But of course all such accounts should finish with a happy ending. While we are all mesmerized by catastrophe, we don't want to make ourselves sound incompetent – so that's why near misses, mistakes that almost happened, and averted catastrophes are the ones to share.

I don't need a new office cleaning company at the moment. But if I do – or if anyone were to ask me for one – I know who I would go to straight away.

So what's your story?

Five damn good stories

Do you have a favorite record? Anything that you've listened to time and again? One of mine is Tchaikovsky's *Romeo and Juliet Fantasy Overture after Shakespeare*. And I've listened to it hundreds of times – uplifting strings and heartrending harmonies that make it my favorite piece of background music while I'm trying to work at my computer.

But much as I love the piece, I don't listen to it all of the time. I can't listen to it all of the time. I like music from Britney Spears to Destiny's Child, Michael Bublé to Carole King. It all depends on my mood.

And the same goes for the people that you meet. Much as they might enjoy your favorite anecdote, they don't want to listen to it all of the time. And it depends on the mood of your conversation with them too.

So you need a handful of good stories to tell. Especially when you are meeting people for a sec.ond or third time. Or think about what happens when you have just told your favorite story to someone, and then another person joins you. Yes, you could repeat the same story to the new person – but then you'd risk boring the first one to tears.

Coming up with interesting stories to tell is easy if you put your mind to it.

Think about the most difficult person you've ever worked with. Who were they? Why were they difficult? And how did you resolve the situation? (Remember to get that happy ending into the story.)

For another anecdote, think about anything you've done at work that you are particularly proud of. Perhaps you received some unexpectedly glowing praise for a piece of work.

Or maybe you have had some dealings with a company that has been in the news (for either positive or negative reasons) lately. People are fascinated by headlines – and even if your interac.tion with the company has been relatively modest, I can guarantee that they will appreciate any insight or intrigue you might be able to share.

When the tone of conversation is less serious, think about anything funny that has ever happened to you. Perhaps you made a (minor) mistake that resulted in you feeling a bit foolish. A case of mistaken identity or sending an email to the wrong person. Maybe a public gaffe. Or an amusing anecdote about how you were nearly late for an important meeting.

For each of these anecdotes, the acronym CAR may help you to structure what you need to say. CAR stands for Challenge, Actions, Result. So think about the challenge that you were faced with – the problem, crisis, difficult colleague, demanding customer, or tricky situation. The A for actions is fairly self-explanatory – what did you do about the challenge? Try to encapsulate in three or four sentences what you did to sort out the challenge. Finally, you need one or at most two sentences to capture the outcome or result that you achieved (satisfied customer, revenues generated, value added, and so on).

CAR gives you the basics of the stories you need to tell. So what would be your fistful of stories?

Be smart, be stupid – but be memorable

"There is only one thing in the world worse than being talked about, and that is not being talked about." Oscar Wilde coined many popular quotes, and I'm a big believer that this is true for aspiring networkers too.

Having a tale to tell is not just about recounting an occurrence from your past. Talking through the challenge, actions, and result will only get you so far. To use an analogy, if you were painting a picture, so far you have only penciled in the outlines. Now it's time to add color.

There is a scene in Raymond Chandler's *The Big Sleep* when hard-boiled detective Philip Marlowe meets the troublemaker of the novel. Carmen Sternwood had "sharp predatory teeth…. They glistened between her thin too taut lips. Her face lacked color and didn't look too healthy."

That's what you need to do in telling your stories. In describing people, try to dramatize your interactions with them. It's the little details that make it memorable. Was your protagonist so nervous he had sweat stains darkening the armpits of his shirt? Did she have a face like she was sucking on lemons? Panicking so much that he was literally shaking? Yelling so forcefully that he was covering your face in spit? Present a caricature of the people you had to deal with.

You need to do more than relate the facts. Emphasize the peril of situations. Exaggerate the circumstances to make it sound important and worth listening to. Inject a sense of jeop.ardy into your tale. After all, having a good story to tell is about making yourself memorable. It's not about being faithful to all of the tedious, minor details.

To sum up, a very famous fellow puts it rather well. Whether he was a military genius and a revolutionary leader or a little dictator, Napoleon Bonaparte captured the art of story telling by saying, "To be believed, make the truth unbelievable."

And one killer question

A good networking encounter should last no more than 15 to 20 minutes. Less isn't enough time to build a rapport. But too long and you are limiting your chances to meet other people who could be even better contacts in the future. Not to mention the fact that the person you are talking to, no matter how polite they seem, may also want to get away to network with other people too.

So there comes a point when you need to ask your penultimate question – whether you can stay in touch. Try something along the lines of: "I'd like to stay in touch if that's all right with you?"

The other person will almost certainly say "Yes." At which point you should ask for their card. Always ask for theirs before offering yours. And only give them your card if they ask for it – otherwise the likelihood is that they will simply take it and consign it to a bin with the rest of the rubbish they receive on a daily basis.

If they don't have a card on them, persist and ask for an email address. Check the spelling carefully as you go along. And jot it down in your notebook. (You need a smart black notebook that fits neatly into an inside jacket pocket or a hand.bag. Get a smart pen too – what kind of impression do you think a disposable biro makes?)

But the killer question isn't whether you can stay in touch. It is to add: "If there's anything of particular interest to you – anything I can keep an eye out for – what would it be?"

The question gives them license to ask you for help. You are making yourself useful; you are offering to fulfill their needs. And by making yourself useful enough times, they will eventually feel that they need to return the favor and help you out.

You might need to prompt them. Having listened to what they have been telling you, might any of the following apply to them?

- Wanting to make money.
- Exploring ways to attract more customers and grow their business.
- Needing to save time or improve efficiency
- looking for a new job – perhaps in a different industry or sector.
- Wanting to gather intelligence about customers or competitors in the marketplace.
- Looking to raise their own profile or perhaps that of their business.

It could take them a few seconds to think about what they are looking for, so be patient. But the answer to that question will be the key to getting in touch again and, most importantly, staying in touch.

The recency effect

First impressions count. There is no doubt about that. If you make a bad first impression, people remember it for a very, very long time.

But last impressions count too. And, lo and behold, pesky psychologists have given it a jumped-up name: "the recency effect."

There's a big chunk of research that backs it up. If you have a 20-minute meeting with someone, they will remember the first couple of minutes and the last minute or so. The middle chunk will blur over time. But those final few seconds really matter.

I always find it a real shame when people depart without thinking about the signals they are sending out. Breaking eye contact and slipping away meekly from a conversation, waving a weak goodbye, or apologizing for having to leave – signals such as these can undermine all of the hard work you have put into building a rapport.

Concentrate on those last few seconds. Focus and don't let your guard down.

Find something positive to say about the other person. For example, a delicate touch of flattery said sincerely rarely goes wrong:

- "It has been genuinely fascinating talking to you. I've learnt a lot about your business and I hope we can keep in touch."
- "I've had so many dull conversations this morning, so it's been great to meet someone who seems to share my sense of humor!"

Or refer back to something that they have been talking about:

- "I think you have a really compelling busi.ness case, so I wish you every success in the coming year."
- "It has been so useful listening to how you have dealt with those operational issues. Do let me know if I can ever return the favor."
- "Good luck with that presentation on Friday. I'm sure it will go smoothly and I'd like to hear all about it sometime."

Then, holding eye contact, give the other person a big smile and a handshake. And then you have completed a successful networking interaction.

Premature congratulation

Don't worry, it happens to every man (and woman) occasionally. We get a little too excited, and then we prematurely congratulate.

It happens when we meet someone who seems entranced by our every utterance. They listen to our introductions and have keen observations on the anecdotes we share with them. They ask questions that show they really understand us. They laugh when they are supposed to. When we hint at our objectives, they are almost grateful to hear more about them.

All of this builds up our confidence and we might be so emboldened that we ask them there and then if they can help us to achieve our objective. Do they know anyone who might have a job for us? Might they be willing to help us raise money for our charitable foundation? Would they let us to speak to their contacts to see if they might be interested in buying our services?

But that would be a big mistake. A huge mistake, in fact. Because your goal in meeting some.one for the first time is simply to build a sufficient rapport to allow you to get in touch with them again in the (near) future. No matter how polite and interested they may seem, they really do not know enough about you to trust you. They might think you are pleasant – but what's in it for them to help you out?

You might appear credible – but are they really going to risk putting their reputation at risk by recommending you to their contacts?

No.

Asking them to help you with your ultimate objective is to waste talking to them. You will scare them off.

Faced with a direct question as to whether they would help with your objective, they might even say yes, they would be willing to help you. But secretly they would be thinking no, no, no, no, no – because they do not want to appear rude in turning you down flat. And when you do make that phone call, you will almost certainly find that their PA keeps telling you that they are busy on other calls. Or if you email, don't hold your breath for a reply, as you could be waiting a very, very long time.

So slow the pace down of your first meeting. Your objective is not to be shared at this stage. Take your time. Make sure that premature congratulation is something that happens to other people – not you.

Mirror, mirror

Isn't it great when you meet someone who has something in common with you? Perhaps they went to the same university; maybe you both worked in a similar role or have a friend in common. You can laugh and cry, commiserate and gossip with them. We instantly find a way to bond with people over aspects of our lives that overlap.

That bonding is critical because, in the average networking conversation of no more than 15 to 20 minutes, we have to make people want to like us and want to keep in touch with us.

But the good news is that even if we do not have any common experiences with another person, we can manipulate them into believing we are like them – and therefore likeable.

Neurolinguistic programming (NLP) teaches us that we can develop rapport by mirroring the behavior of other people. By behavior, I don't just mean body language, but also their facial mannerisms and tone and pace of their voice. Used well, it is a technique that can build rapport and enhance communication – without the other person noticing.

The next time you meet someone, observe them and try to incorporate their style into your behavior. Do they make many or very few hand gestures? If they make a lot, then try to emphasize your points with your hands too. Using your hands too much when someone else is very still will seem jarring to them.

Or if you are introduced to someone who proceeds to sit down and slouch into a very relaxed position, it's probably a good idea to sit in a relaxed manner too. Sitting upright with perfect posture could draw attention to you for the wrong reasons.

Listen to the pace and tone of their speech as well. Is it fast and excited or measured with thoughtful pauses between sentences? Try to speed up or down to match the people you meet.

How about their facial expressions? Are they very expressive – flashing their eyes and using wild expressions to illustrate their stories? Or do they communicate in a cooler, calmer, much more businesslike manner?

All of these cues can be incorporated into your behavior to nudge the development of rapport in the right direction. However, the aim is not to form a literal mirror by copying their every nuance and movement. If you were to cross your legs every time they cross their legs, or to scratch your face every time they do so, they will almost certainly detect what you are trying to do and possibly even think that you are laughing at their mannerisms.

Abort, abort, abort!

Ever get stuck with the most boring person in the room? Quiet and avoiding eye contact, seemingly uninterested in you – even when you ask them questions about themselves, they are likely to give monosyllabic answers that serve only to kill the conversation.

The bad news is that you are likely to encounter people just like them on your networking journey. The good news though is that you can take steps to escape them. Unless you are trapped by having to sit next to them at a formal event – which simply is not the case at most networking events, cocktail parties, and the like – you can extract yourself.

The best way to remove yourself is to introduce a third person into the conversation. When the alarm bells are ringing that someone is going to waste your time, try to identify someone else in the room who is on their own.

Suggest to your conversational companion that you involve the third person in the conversation. "Isn't it awful when you come to a conference/party/workshop and you don't know anyone to talk to? Shall we introduce ourselves to that person over there?"

Then approach the third person, introducing yourself and the person you are trying to get rid of. Ask the third person some questions and look for anything that the two people you have just introduced might have in common. Even if it is a fairly tangential commonality, it is better than nothing. "Jane, it's interesting that you work in finance. Peter works in sales for his company. I guess sales and finance are often at odds in most businesses?"

Find a topic that allows the two of them to talk without your input. And once you have allowed them to enter into that conversation, you can excuse yourself without making a fuss.

There are other devious and slightly underhand tactics. One is to look at your watch and explain that you had promised to make a phone call at a particular time. Another is to excuse yourself to refresh your drink. Or ask where the toilets are.

But be careful not to excuse yourself too early. Premature extrication is another problem for many would-be networkers. And a common mistake is to equate a dull personality with being a poor choice of contact. Just because someone is boring does not mean that they may not have a significant budget or important contacts of their own.

In fact, the only people that you should discount are the ones who might have the same networking goal as you.

For example, if you are a freelance graphic artist looking for clients and meet another freelance graphic artist, the two of you are essentially competing to find clients. So make your apologies and take your leave. On the other hand, if you are a sales manager at a conference for sales people, then talking to other sales managers – even if they are also looking for jobs – might provide you with valuable information about the market.

Give everyone an equal chance – spend at least five or ten minutes asking them about their job, their business, their aspirations, and so on. Only when you are sure that there would be no merit in keeping in touch should you hit the abort button.

Card conventions

Not everyone has a business card. But not having one creates a particular impression about you. Others will think that you are too junior and/or unimportant to warrant your employer giving you one. Or they will think that you are lazy and ill-prepared – not the sort of person they would want to stay in touch or do business with.

So get a business card.

Most people use the card that their employer provides them with. However, if you are a free.lance worker or not currently employed, you may want to create your own cards.

Even if an employer provides you with one, you might decide to get a set of personal cards printed. If you are intending to leave your current employer to join another organization or set up your own business, it would be wise to provide contacts with a personal mobile number and email address.

When putting together a business card, less really is more. Keep it simple. Choose plain black text in a conservative font on a sheet of plain white card. And ask your printer for the standard size and thickness of business cards.

Keep the business card as plain as possible unless you have the budget to pay a professional designer to create a layout for you. Networking is about connecting with people because they like and trust you – not because you have a fancy business card. If you are depending on the design of your card to make others remember you, then you have lost the whole point of networking. You are the product that they should remember and be recommending to their contacts – not your business card.

Have the minimum of information on your card. The essentials are nothing more than: your name, job title (or three- to five-word description of the type of work you do), address, telephone number, mobile phone number, and personal email address. If you have a fax number or a pro.fessionally designed website, then those can be added too.

Be careful not to provide too many details on a card. Pager numbers and personal phone num.bers, your secretary's number and so on – these serve only to give the impression that you are a difficult person to get hold of, which could easily put someone off from trying at all. So don't add them. I'm a big fan of the KISS principle – Keep It Simple, Stupid.

Some people have tag lines or personal statements on their cards that are intended to remind the person taking your card what you do. But as many people loathe them as like them. So why take the risk? Leave this off your card too.

The final comment I shall make about business cards is to store them properly. I meet a distressingly high proportion of people who keep them in purses or wallets along with their cash and credit cards, or in top jacket pockets or back trouser pockets – which predictably causes the corners of the card to fray or the whole card to take on the shape of their buttocks! Then the person giving me the card inevitably has to apologize about the state of their card, creating the impression that they are a bit disorganized. You don't need to buy an expensive case in which to carry your cards – even a plastic card holder would do – but make sure you have a sure-fire way to keep them from being damaged.

Having said all that about the importance of having a card, it is more important to get other people's cards than it is for you to give out your own. Then you can decide when and how to get in touch rather than wait on them and risk them losing your card.

Glad to see the back of them

Business cards have another vital function. They are the perfect size for you to scrawl a handful of bullet points on the back of them about the person you have just met.

A good networking event might present you with the opportunity to meet dozens of people. At a two- or three-day conference, you could easily meet a hundred or more people. And if you get cards from even just a quarter of them, I would put money on the fact that you won't remember them all.

A business card is perfect for note taking because you are not looking to write an essay. Writing too much could be wasting valuable time when you could be shaking hands and introducing yourself to yet more people. And sometimes you meet people under the strangest of circumstances and may not have a notepad with which to take more comprehensive notes.

I usually make two sorts of notes on the backs of cards. First, I jot down one or two points about why they might be of interest. For example, they might have a budget to buy services, or have influence over the person who does. Perhaps they have contacts that you would be interested in talking to. You might not even have a particularly good reason for keeping in touch with them, other than the fact that they are an influential or senior individual that you want to keep in touch with – just in case.

Second, I scrawl a line or two about what they are looking for. What could you do for them – in order to build up your favor bank?

Focus on rapport

To finish off this section of the book, consider your goal in networking. Yes, you may have a long-term objective, but your short-term goal is to build rapport. Nothing else. Success at network.ing events is not measured by the number of cards that you have managed to exchange. Neither is it measured by the number of people you have met.

It is easy to race round a networking event and give out cards in the same manner as companies send out junk mail. Most junk mail gets binned – and the same will go for your card unless you choose to give it out only to people that you have built a rapport with.

Meeting someone for the first time is all about building enough rapport that they like you and allow you to get in touch with them again. It is about the quality of your interactions rather than the quantity.

Helen Vandevelde, a conference presenter and writer, shares a cautionary tale:

> I was at this networking event, chatting naturally with two new contacts when a woman butted into our conversation. No waiting for a lull in which to introduce her.self, but straight in while we were talking. "I'm Alice and I'm a marketing consultant. How about you?" Well, our group was stunned. So much so that we fell into intro.ducing ourselves. She quickly concluded that none of us was any use to her and moved on. The rest of us exchanged glances and we were fascinated to study her in action. She flitted from one group to the next like a butterfly. Others looked astonished as we had been. She made her aggressive introduction, looked mildly interested for a couple of seconds,

dished out her business cards and then moved
on to the next group. She didn't notice people
crumpling her business cards though.

You often meet networking butterflies like that. And the
problem is that when they do meet someone that they
deem "useful," they stick to them like limpets on a rock,
monopolizing their time and questioning them and trying
to sell themselves in a frankly slightly scary fashion.

So I shall say it again. The initial stage of networking
is about building rapport. It is about being interested and
interesting. The selling of your product, your company, or
yourself comes much, much later. You have been warned.

03

Common Circumstances and Strange Situations

Just about the only place that I wouldn't recommend trying to network is in a communal changing room. Whether they are trying on clothes at the back of a shop or changing at the gym, half-naked people never feel at their most confident.

But in this section, here are some of the other venues and locations in which you should definitely consider networking.

Conference etiquette

Most networkers think about conferences and trade shows when they are asked to picture networking events. And conferences are easy to network at because people are often more interested in the networking opportunities than in visiting exhibitors' stands or listening to keynote speeches.

The commonest convention at conferences is that you will be presented with a name badge at registration.

Now, the mavericks amongst you may be tempted not to wear it. I know some people like to express their individuality. "I am an individual, I am not one of the mindless drones circulating at this event."

I would agree that not wearing your badge certainly does send out a certain message. Unfortunately, it is the wrong message to send out. It tells people that you should not be approached. If you are not wearing a badge, people might wonder whether you are a conference delegate or not. Perhaps you are a conference organizer rather than a delegate. Are you maybe a well-dressed security guard or there only to serve teas and coffees?

Even if the name badge spells your name or company name incorrectly – which many do, such is the level of disorganization and ineptitude with which so many conferences are orchestrated – I would recommend wearing your badge anyway. Take a pen and correct the spelling and wear it. If it is an amusing spelling mistake, it might even form the basis for a talking point when you meet new people.

Pin your badge on your right lapel, gentlemen, or the right side of your blouse, ladies. Why the right side? Because when you shake hands with someone, your eyes are naturally drawn to their right hand and the right side of their body.

Making the most of conferences

Conferences take time to organize – even the shoddy ones that you visit once and then wish you had not bothered with.

But the fact that conference organizers book speakers and put together delegate lists many months in advance can be used to your benefit. If you are a novice networker, you may be happy to arrive at a conference and simply allow chance to dictate the people that you meet. However, if you are keen to further your objective, you may decide to target your attention more keenly at conferences.

It is certainly a tactic recommended by veteran networkers such as Linda Kennedy, HR director at support services company Cleanaway and Brambles Industrial Services:

> Try to get the list of attendees and companies before the event you are attending. Review it fairly thoroughly and mark off the people that you specifically want to talk to. This could be because they are relevant to your business, a recognized authority in a certain field, or have done work in an area of common interest.
>
> At the event, be focused on getting around at least your top five people. Think about what you want to get out of the discussion beforehand and think about what you could offer them, by way of common ground, best practice, or any other anecdotes that might be of interest. It is very easy to revert to talking with existing contacts or friends – so make the effort to establish new contacts at every event you attend.

Wanting to meet speakers – as opposed to other delegates – at the conference requires essentially the same tactic.

However, be aware that speakers are usually inundated by requests and invitations to meet them. Don't be surprised after their presentation if there is a queue of people waiting to talk to them. If you join the queue, you will probably have only two or three minutes to make an impact. So make sure that you have a truly compelling reason for them to want to speak to you.

Are you carrying an offensive weapon?

Mobile phones are simultaneously one of the greatest developments of the 20th century (who would have thought even 20 years ago that we would all be able to keep in touch pretty much wherever we are on the planet?) and the greatest bane of our existence (isn't it annoying when they go off in meetings and, even worse, the person then proceeds to take the call?)

Switch your mobile phone or pager off. If you absolutely must have them on, put them onto silent vibrate mode. And only do so if you are expecting an important call or message. Rarely can a caller not wait 20 minutes until you have finished speaking to someone for you to check your messages and call them back.

Briefcases, laptop bags, and handbags can also, inadvertently, be offensive weapons at networking events. It is a small tip, but if you must carry one, do so on the left-hand side of your body. This allows you to meet new people and shake hands with your right hand without disrupting your serene manner by first having to transfer a bag to the other shoulder or a briefcase or handbag to the other hand.

Talking business

Many organizations invite guests to attend evening events that might at first seem to be social occasions. Perhaps the invitation is to visit a gallery and peruse the works of a new artist or sample vintages from a wine cellar. Drinks and canapés, a buffet, or even a sit-down dinner might be on offer. But no matter what guise they take, these are all really business events masquerading as social events. No organization is selfless enough to offer something for nothing after all.

In fact, the sponsoring organization almost certainly has an agenda of its own – and you must respect it in order to play the part of a good guest. The sponsor might, for example, have a number of speakers during the evening or expect you to watch a video presentation. No matter how boring these are, you must pay attention – as someone you meet later could ask your point of view on it. They might have an exhibition on display that you are expected to look at. Or there could be a raffle to raise money for a specified charity – take your lead from other people and make sure that you buy a similar number of tickets to avoid looking cheap.

Evening events are not intended for blatant selling or self-promotion. However, they are still opportunities to network. Do not reveal your objective. But do approach people and work on building up a sufficient level of rapport to be able to ask if you can keep in touch with them.

The best icebreaker for any business event is to start the conversation off by referring to the purpose of the event.

If, for example, the event is aimed at raising money for a particular charity, it might be appropriate to comment on a surprising fact that you did not know about the charity or their aims.

If you are attending an event designed to promote a new product, then make some comment about the sponsoring organization and how the new product might help that organization to meet its stated goals. At meetings organized by a professional association, it might be appropriate simply to ask how other people are getting on in their organizations. If you are attending a book launch, ask whether they know the author or have read any of their other works. Or ask how the other person came to be invited to the event and explore that connection for a few minutes.

Alumni gatherings are becoming increasingly popular too. Schools and universities often use them as a means of raising funds for big projects. A growing number of businesses also use them as a way to develop their brand and raise their profile amongst ex-employees. If you arrive at an alumni event and find that there are very few or even no people there that you recognize, then a good icebreaker is to ask when someone graduated/left the organization. Again, the key is to look for something that you both have in common that could form the basis for a relationship.

Networking while nibbling

An international team of scientists conducting a five-year study into spaghetti consumption have found that 73.6

percent of spaghetti eaters end up splattering their clothes with tomato sauce.

Okay, so I made up that statistic. And, if you hadn't guessed already, there never was any such study (or at least none that I know of – please let me know if there is). But eating during networking events – breakfast meetings, power lunches, conference buffets, and client parties – can be a minefield for the unwary.

The easiest way to negotiate the treacherous territory of eating and networking is to keep the two separate. If you are going to an event at which you hope to make a lot of contacts, then maybe avoid the food all together and eat before you arrive.

Cocktail parties and buffets are particularly tricky for the novice networking nibbler. A plate in one hand, a drink in the other, and suddenly someone approaches you with arm outstretched to shake your hand! And even if you do manage to free a hand without dropping your plate or drink, chances are that your fingers will be covered in grease.

At stand-up buffets or drinks and canapé evenings, some experienced networkers recommend that you do not eat, and carry only a drink in your left hand, leaving your (clean) right hand free to shake hands with people. Or eat near a table so that you are able to put your plate down and pick up your glass – but never have both in your hands at the same time.

Personally, I prefer to enjoy myself if the food is good – but admittedly I do run the risk of having a mouthful of chicken satay and my fingers clasped round a greasy skewer when the CEO of my target business walks past me. But you are an adult and can make up your own mind about whether you want to risk eating and drinking and networking at the same time.

Alcohol is another temptation that can be even more fatal. That most respected icon of our times, Homer Simpson, once said: "Homer no function beer well without." But unless you are an incompetent alcoholic cartoon character with a habit for strangling his son and insulting the neighbors, you might be better off networking by the motto, "You no function beer well with." So know your limit. As with all drugs, alcohol can give you the illusion of feeling more erudite and interesting. But the reality is that you are probably slurring your words, turning pink-faced, and talking rubbish. So make that trade off – are you at a net.working event to have a good time or meet people who might be useful? The two are mutually incompatible.

Plane speaking
The best thing about networking with passengers on a flight is that they are a captive audience!

It is even better if you are traveling business class. You get more than just a free glass of champagne, as the business-class cabin will be packed with middle and senior managers – men and women with budgets, contacts, and influence.

It really does happen, as Toni Castle, Global Client Services Director at public relations agency LEWIS, relates:

Having not had a holiday all year, I took the opportunity to head to New Zealand in November to switch off completely. The daunting prospect of a thirteen-hour flight to Singapore followed immediately by another ten hours to the final destination was pretty much the only thing on my mind.

I thought nothing of smiling in acknowledgement at the person in the seat next to me as I sat down on the plane. The conversation started, as would any other with a stranger going on holiday: "Are you going to Singapore on business?" "No, I'm taking a break from work in New Zealand." "Oh, what do you do?" "PR." "That's interesting, my company is looking for a PR agency."

That's all it took. I didn't know I would be sitting next to the CEO of a potential client on that trip. I found myself present.ing my company's credentials, delivering initial PR campaign ideas, and agreeing next steps with a new business prospect – all from my seat. My agency ultimately secured the business too.

So how do you do it?

If you arrive at your seat to find a person already sat in the seat next to yours, begin by making eye contact, smiling and saying "Hello." After storing any hand luggage in the overhead compartment, take out a book, newspaper, or business magazine, and settle into your seat.

If you are already seated when someone arrives, then make eye contact, smile, and say "Hello." Allow the other person to store hand luggage and get settled while you peruse your book or magazine.

The reading material is important because it sends out a signal. It tells the other person that you have something to do – you are not intending to monopolize their time for the entire flight. The conversation you are about to initiate is merely a minor diversion before you return to your reading.

And then your icebreaker is to ask: "Are you returning home or about to travel to a meeting?"

The rest is up to you.

The same technique can be used on trains too. But on trains with unassigned seating, you can pick your target much more carefully. Look for lone travelers wearing suits. But avoid travelers who have already powered up their laptops and spread a sheaf of documents on the table, as they probably have too much work to do to want to talk.

Back on the plane, however, the fact that they are unable to escape physically means that you need to be much more careful in trying to network with them. Attending a trade show or conference implies that you are willing to be approached by would-be networkers. But on a plane, many people want nothing more than peace and quiet to work or sleep. As such, pay close attention to their body language and level of interest. Poor eye contact or non-committal replies might be a signal for you to stop.

If you are at all uncertain about interpreting the complex dance that is body language, then the "20 twice" rule might help you to read the other person.

When a natural break arises in the conversa.tion, break eye contact and count to 20 in your head. Count slowly. Don't rush.

If they have not spoken by the time you have reached 20, it may be a signal that they are not interested in pursuing the conversation. On the other hand, they might be quite enjoying the conversation, but a bit shy, and unable to think of another topic with which to reinvigorate the discussion. So that's when you allow yourself to ask a question about another topic.

But when another natural break crops up in the conversation, count slowly to 20 for a second time. If they do not pick up the discussion, then take it as a signal that they would rather not continue.

Four weddings and a funeral

Thrusting your business card at the grieving widow at a funeral probably isn't the best idea in the world. But networking opportunities can crop up in most gatherings.

Weddings can be great networking opportunities, as can anniversary and birthday celebrations, and housewarming and cocktail parties.

Overt networking at social occasions will horrify people. They are there to enjoy themselves and there are conventions about such occasions. At a wedding, for example, you are there to celebrate the joining of two people to each other.

The great thing about weddings is that you are not only allowed, but actively encouraged, to speak to people you do not know. A great ice.breaker is to ask how people know the couple. The same goes for just about any social occasion – ask how they know the host or guest of honor.

Always spend a few minutes sharing anecdotes about the couple, host, or guest of honor. And concentrate on being a good guest – laugh at their jokes and look as if you are enjoying the event. While you are being a good guest, though, listen out for opportunities to gently steer the discussion onto business-related topics. For example:

You: "So how do you know the birthday boy?"

Guest: "We went to university together."

You: "You must have some stories to tell then!"

Guest: "Yes ..." (goes on to relate a couple of stories)

You: "It sounds like you had a great time together. I know he studied finance at university. Is that how you know each other?"

Guest: "No, we shared a house together. I studied physics."

You: "And do you now work in that field?"

Guest: "No, I left and retrained as a lawyer."

Ker-ching! You have managed to nudge the conversation onto a business topic.

Be careful not to push too hard, though. If you ask too many questions about the nature of their work and their business, you will almost certainly give the impression that you are an over-ambitious networker who is at the event only to use people.

Focus instead on building a rapport with people. If the other person does not seem too interested in talking business at a social event, you should allow the conversation to drift onto other topics. It is more important to make the other person feel that they like you and would want to speak to you again than it is to probe them for information and specific opportunities.

You can always ask your mutual friend for their phone number or email address and pick up the conversation at a later, more appropriate time.

So just as "any time, any place, anywhere" used to be the slogan of Martini, it should be your slogan when it comes to networking.

Meetings, meetings, meetings

Meetings are like visits to the dentist. Everyone moans about having to attend them, but we grudgingly acknowledge that we probably need them.

Meetings are especially important if you are employed, as opposed to being self-employed. For some unfathomable reason, many people perceive networking to be something that happens outside their day-to-day jobs. People who are employees often discount the fact that they have access to an immense internal network.

But for the aspiring networker, meetings are one of the commonest opportunities to meet people and forge new relationships. Another common misconception is that networking goes on mainly at trade shows and conferences, but the reality is that most of us do not get to attend that many of them – perhaps no more than a couple every month. Compare that with the many meetings you attend in just one week.

In order to use meeting time well, take note of new people that you meet. When someone arrives at a meeting that you have not met, make the effort to approach them and introduce yourself.

Introduce yourself by explaining your role in the meeting. Most of the time, your introduction should consist of your name and your job title. For example, when meeting an external person, someone might say: "Hi, I'm Steve Jefferson. I'm the account director at Smith Hewitt Partners."

If you have a specific role in the meeting, then it might be appropriate to add a sentence about that role: "Hello, I'm Jennifer Clayton. I'm the head buyer and I'll be leading the presentation on customer trends this season."

After they have introduced themselves, segue immediately onto a couple of neutral questions that will encourage them to talk further, for example, "How long have you worked here?" followed by, "And what was your background before joining XYZ company?"

Meeting etiquette dictates that you wait until you are seated before exchanging business cards. But only do this if you are meeting with people external to your organization – clients or customers, suppliers or business partners.

During the meeting, take notes about the people in the room. Capture a couple of points about what they want to get out of the meeting, but also write down any interesting facts you discover that would help you to get back in touch with them. For example, someone at a meeting recently joked that he was not going to be involved in the initial stages of the project because he was about to go to the Maldives on holiday. That fact alone was enough to form the basis for an informal email later when I wanted to get in touch.

If you are one of those (rare) people who feels that you are not invited to enough meetings, then start to volunteer. Ask managers if you can take part in cross-functional projects, committees, working parties, and change programs. Most organizations have a raft of projects and not enough people to do them, so your offer to help will almost certainly be warmly received.

Become a center of attention

Speaking at conferences, presenting at seminars – even giving a talk at an internal meeting – is a powerful way for growing your network. Speakers draw attention to themselves, and so long as you have something worthwhile that others want to hear, people in the audience are bound to approach you with questions. Even better, being a speaker is the ultimate networking icebreaker – it gives you license to circulate amongst the audience and talk to anyone you like.

Giving formal presentations can feel very daunting – even senior managers often avoid doing it and pay professionals to coach them on how to do it better. But it really is a case of feeling the fear and doing it anyway. JFDI. No one is saying that you have to start as the keynote speaker at an international conference. Start small – perhaps by giving talks at discussion groups with.in your organization. Make sure that you attend the events run by your professional association, observe the speakers there, then put in a bid to speak at a future event too.

Speaking at events generates a buzz. If you present well, people will remember you and invite you to speak at other events. But that is a big "if" – and in order to do it well, focus equally on the "three Ps" of presenting: preparation, practice, and performance.

The preparation element requires time to plan what you will say. Write out what you will say. If you need to write PowerPoint slides, create any diagrams, or organize handouts, make sure that you do this well in advance. What questions are people likely to ask? And how would you answer those? Include your contact details on your slides or handouts so that people can reach you afterwards too. As a rule of thumb, be ready to spend three times as long preparing as you will take in presenting – a one-hour talk could easily take three hours to plan.

The next step is to practice, practice, practice. Again, as a rule of thumb, spend two to three times as long practicing as your planned presenta.tion time. You will probably find that, as you go through the presentation, you may wish to change sentences that sound clumsy, delete material that does not seem entirely relevant, or add further explanations to make it flow better. A colleague of mine takes his presentations home and talks through important presentations to his cat. I take mine home and, standing at one end of my lounge, stare down the 20-foot length of the room through the windows, pretending that I am making eye contact with the people at the back of the auditorium. When people go wrong in presentations, it is usually because they have not practiced saying it out loud enough times.

And so onto the third element – the perform.ance. Presenting well is not simply reading out your prepared script. It's a good idea to think of yourself as an actor who needs to perform in order to hold the attention of your entire audi.ence. I'm sure you have seen speakers who stand at a lectern and speak in a monotone voice – it's hardly an engaging performance. Think about the good speakers that you have seen. They move around the room and use expansive gestures. They use their tone of voice – raising it to indicate excitement and lowering it to talk about problems or difficulties. They pause in a dramatic fashion in order to allow the audience to ponder key points.

It is beyond the scope of this section to discuss good presentation skills – it is a book in its own right. But so long as you focus on the three Ps, you will deliver effective presentations and make people want to talk to you.

Networking and career support groups

While Sex Addicts Anonymous may not be quite the right venue for networking (do email me if you have any stories to say otherwise though – I'll put it in the next edition of the book!), there are many groups set up to support networking between professionals with a particular interest or background.

Networks exist for women, ethnic minorities, religious groups, parents, and gays and lesbians. Support groups also exist for people who have been made redundant. Different ages are also well represented – with groups targeting young people seeking employment as well as older people who may have experienced age discrimination. There are also groups for people who have medical conditions. The specified purpose of many of these groups is to further career development. Other groups are less specific, and mention only that their aims are to "support" each other – and who is to say that the form of that support cannot be to promote each other's careers?

As just one example, typing the words "women," "network," and "UK" into a search engine located hundreds of groups. The first page of results alone included the Women's Business Network, for businesswomen in the northwest of England, and the Rural Women's Network for women in Cumbria looking to set up their own businesses.

Many businesses also set up internal groups as part of their efforts to promote diversity. Management consultancy the Boston Consulting Group has a Gay and Lesbian Network spanning its 60 worldwide offices, which provides mentor.ing to consultants, has quarterly conference calls, and an annual retreat. American Express has the Black Employee Network for its African– American employees. Pharmaceutical giant GlaxoSmithKline has an Asian Employee Support Group.

Such groups are easy to locate on the Internet and are almost always happy to accept visitors to meetings. By virtue of the fact that you share an interest or perhaps your heritage with the people in such a networking group, these groups provide relatively safe environments for you to practice your networking skills. And, who knows? You might make a few very useful contacts too.

04

Nurture your Network

Whether you have managed to collect one card or a hundred, your efforts will go to waste if you don't follow up. The initial meeting and greeting stage of networking is only the first in a series of steps. Any semi-articulate idiot can go to a networking event and gather a pile of business cards. It takes effort and persistence to turn those business contacts into useful business resources.

Keep tally

The scribbled note on the back of a business card is a start. But dedicated networkers will make more detailed notes to help them remember the people they have met.

You could keep written notes, but most net-workers find it easier to use a database or spread.sheet. Programs such as Microsoft Outlook have a "Contacts" function that allows you to input notes alongside people's address and contact details. Even a simple text document would suffice to capture everything you can remember about them.

Do a "brain dump" of as much as you can remember about that person. Personal background is as important as information about the person's job or organization. No matter how vividly you remember someone at a given moment in time, the details will inevitably fade. Following up effectively requires that you can refer to details about other people correctly. Imagine how unimpressed you would be if someone got in touch with you and spelt the name of your partner wrongly or misremembered where you used to work.

Here are some examples of the biographies of people that I have made after an initial meeting:

> Director of strategy at DEF plc. Formerly interim head of strategy and development at the ABC company (from Feb to Aug 2005). Prior to that worked in oil and gas (can't remember – where?). She went to Cuba on holiday after leaving ABC and before joining DEF plc in September. Currently has two direct reports but needs to recruit one more. Says that her first project is to manage the integration of a German acquisition into the business. She bought a house in west London with her partner in spring/summer 2004, with a 30-foot garden.
>
> Met her at AHAA event 16 July 2004. She used to work at Ogilvy & Mather as planning director. Five years ago she quit to set up a business doing facilitation and group work, some training. She suggested there might

be some opportunities to refer one-to-one coaching and assessment work on to me. Dark hair, wore glasses, late 30s/ early 40s.

Met him at Recruitment International show on 5 January 2005. He has been chief executive of recruitment consultancy JKL for five years. I was presenting alongside of Mark Lewis from the Genesis Trust. He gave me his card and said that his company do not currently have a senior level assess.ment product. I think they do assessment for more junior levels though? His surname Kohan is pronounced "Co-en" (silent "h"). Grey-haired, mid-40s, quite overweight, he has an American (or is it Canadian?) accent.

Sometimes the description may be very work-oriented; other times the focus may be more on personal interests. As you can see from my examples, not all of the details are politically correct. I'm sure that my age estimations could be out by up to a decade in some cases. And if anyone ever knew that I'd written down that they were overweight, it would do me no favors. But I find that the more detail I capture, the more able I am to summon up what they look and sound like, which in turn helps me to prepare for getting in touch with them.

Assume at your peril
Another point that many of us have learnt by hard experience is that everyone can potentially be important.

It's easy to assume that certain people are more important than others – and most of the time you will be right.

"I have tended to write off some people as soon as I meet them for a combination of reasons," admits Marc Kitten, a partner at strategic consultancy Candesic. "It can be down to intellectual laziness, general tiredness, a lack of immediate common interests, or because I am more interested by the buffet. Like many other people, I am unconsciously attracted in priority to those who are good-looking, tall, healthy, wealthy, outgoing, proficient speakers, and so on."

But beware of appearances. As the saying goes, they can be deceptive.

"At a cocktail party I once overlooked a badly-shaved, poorly-dressed guy who was talking to a good-looking female colleague of mine," continues Kitten. "I thought she needed help to escape and took her away without much warning. She angrily pushed me away and I discovered that he was the new president of a central bank – a potentially huge customer."

The same goes for the notes that you make. I used to make notes only on the people that I assumed were "important" to save time. In retrospect, I was lazy.

But it could be a very big mistake to make.

For a start, your objective may change as time goes by. Mine has changed in just a few years. When I was happily employed by a consultancy, my objective was to sell consulting services to people who would buy large projects of many tens of thousands of pounds in value and over. So I used to make notes only on people I met who I thought might have substantial budgets of their own. In the last couple of years, an ex-colleague and I decided to set up our own consulting business, so I am now on the lookout for more modestly sized projects. Unfortunately, I never kept records of the many managers that I met – many of whom might have had discretion over smaller budgets.

As another example, I have the privilege of working with banking giant HSBC. I met one of their managers about 18 months ago, but she was not the project manager or the budget holder, so I did not bother to make any notes on her. A year later, I received a call from her. The name has been changed to protect my dignity, but the exchange is real: "Hello, it's Kelly Ashford at HSBC here. How are you?"

I had no idea who she was and must have sounded a bit confused. She asked, "Do you remember who I am?" and I have to admit that I lied and said "Yes." I managed to keep the conversation going, and she offered me a piece of work. But it could all have gone horribly wrong because I had assumed that she was not "important" enough to warrant keeping tabs on.

There is a saying that you should never assume, because it makes an ASS out of U and ME, and this was certainly true for me. I'm not saying that you need to write an essay on everyone. Just their name, phone number, and a few lines on each would do.

Not every event is important

There are only 24 hours in the day and 365 days in the year. So unless you don't plan on sleeping in the next year or two, you may want to prioritize the events that you decide to visit. Especially as some of the bigger and more prestigious industry events require payment of not insubstantial sums.

Linda Kennedy, HR director at Cleanaway and Brambles Industrial Services, agrees about the need to prioritize:

> Target the events you wish to attend. Your time is precious and each minute spent should be value adding.
>
> Do an assessment of each event once you have attended it, and make notes on what you got out of it, who you met, and whether you would attend again. For example, there is a big annual HR event on the cruise ship Aurora, but it is probably only worth attending every three or four years. It may sound a bit too systematic but it doesn't take long, and will be much better than trying to rely on your memory.

The three-day rule

You cannot expect the people you meet to remember you forever based on only one short meeting. Very few people are diligent at following up, so it is probably a safe bet that they have not gone away and made notes about you.

In order to reinforce the rapport that you have established face-to-face, you should aim to make contact with people. But there is an optimum window within which you should aim to get in touch.

Getting in touch is a bit like dating. If you get in touch too quickly, then you could make the other person think that you are too keen. Think Glenn Close in the movie *Fatal Attraction* – her character was a bit too keen. And look at all the trouble she caused Michael Douglas's character. It didn't end well for her either.

The reason why we must never seem too eager is that when it comes to building new relationships we need to respect the unspoken rules of business. One of these rules is that we must always seem to be busy. Most managers and executives usually are incredibly busy. In order to create the impression that we are like them, we must also appear to be busy – even if it means having to delay a task that we might actually have the time to do immediately.

Waiting for too long to get in touch has obvious drawbacks. Your contact could simply forget who you are, or why they might have wanted to stay in touch with you.

As a rule of thumb, leave it at least two or three days, but no more than a couple of weeks at the most.

Pick up a pen

A client of mine once complained that she had accumulated 492 email messages in her inbox while she had been on holiday for just one week. Most of them were completely irrelevant – about servers that had crashed and then further emails about the status of the crashed server before a final email reporting that the service had finally been restored.

Then there were emails from colleagues who had "kindly" decided to c.c. her in case she might be interested – and in most cases she was most certainly not interested.

And that isn't even that many emails. I know that the marketing team at California-based Veritas Software easily notch up about 300 emails in a single day.

It should therefore come as no surprise that email is not the best medium for making the first follow-up. Skimming through dozens of email messages, mouse hovering over the delete key, it can be easy for someone to delete your email message – no matter how carefully composed, informative, and useful it might be.

A telephone call is harder to ignore, but can be rather presumptuous for an initial follow-up unless you have something of real and immediate importance to impart. I would generally wait until the second or perhaps third follow-up before using the telephone.

While people moan about the number of emails they have to sort through and can find phone calls from relative strangers intrusive, I have never heard a single person complain about receiving handwritten notes from people that they know.

In fact, I can still remember the last handwritten note that I received. It was over a year ago, after meeting Viv Du-Feu, Head of the Human Resources Group at law firm Eversheds, for the first time. He believes – as do I – that in an age of instantaneous communications and declining standards of care and courtesy, an old-fashioned handwritten note goes a long way to separate you from the rest.

I almost can't believe that it has been over a year since I last received a handwritten note. Why are people so lazy?

Your note need not be complicated. Begin by referring to the event that you attended, for example: "It was good to meet you at the Health & Safety Seminar last week."

Go on to mention something of interest that the person said or that you both had in common: "I think we both agreed that the speakers were of a rather variable quality! So I was very glad to have met someone who had some more practical ideas to share." Or make a comment about the person if you can say something genuine: "It was refreshing to hear you speak so candidly about the difficulties you experienced in implementing the project."

And then refer back to anything that they said would be of interest to them: "If I come across anyone who is looking out for someone with your skills, I shall be sure to put the two of you in contact."

I usually finish by reminding them of my con.tact details: "Do let me know if I can ever help in any way. Give me a ring on my mobile 07955 100 300 or drop me an email to rob@organisation.name.com."

An example note to someone who has given you some help finding a new job might go as follows:

> Thank you for spending a few minutes with me the other day. I thought your comments were very useful and I shall be hoping to put your advice into action very soon. I'm not sure how I can return the favor, but if you can think of

anything, don't hesitate to pick up the phone to 030 8742 1500 or feel free to email me at: ry@emailaddress.com.

Your entire letter needs only to be four or five sentences long.

Be careful about enclosing additional materials in this first correspondence. If the person expressed interest about a particular paper you have written or a newspaper article, then it would be appropriate to enclose it. However, it always annoys people when they receive a brochure or a catalog that they had not asked for. Even a handwritten note alongside your sales material will make it no more palatable. Networking is a gradual process of building up relationships that will enable you to ask for favors – it is not the same as pushing your services onto people at the first opportunity.

P.S.

Networking is all about building up warm relationships with people. Sometimes it is worth reminding your contacts that you are paying attention not only to what they do – their role, responsibility, and business – but also to who they are – their personality, their activities and interests outside of work, and their families.

Whether you are getting in touch by hand.written note or later by email, the postscript allows you to remind them in the briefest of fashions, without reducing the impact of your main message.

Some examples:

- P.S. Have a great time in New York.
- P.S. Good luck with the exam – I've got my fingers crossed for you.
- P.S. Hope you enjoy the movie this week.end – let me know what you think!

Try it.

The next step

A handwritten note will win you points for the fact that it is so remarkable in today's fast-paced, high-tech world. But you are only as memorable as your last missive. Networking is not a process that is ever complete – it needs constant effort and attention. Contacts will forget you if you stop getting in touch with them.

Try to follow up again within a matter of months in order to refresh their memories and keep you at the forefront of their minds. While it is perfectly permissible to send a thank you note as a first follow-up, your second follow-up should ideally be more relevant or thought-provoking. And now that you have made the effort with one handwritten note, you should allow yourself the luxury of adding the telephone and email as means of keeping in touch. Even the occasional text message might be appropriate for a time-critical announcement.

Look out for articles or items of news that might be relevant to each of your contacts. Is there a newspaper article or magazine clipping mention.ing their company, or perhaps discussing their industry, that you could send them? You could even send a short email with a hyperlink to a web page that they might be interested in reading.

Consider the seminars, conferences, and other events that you are invited to – might there be anything that someone in your network might be interested in? If you look hard enough, it can be quite fascinating, as you may discover that what you would disregard as junk mail could be incredibly relevant to someone you know.

I often get in touch with contacts on the basis of having encountered other people in a similar role or the same industry. Perhaps you could make some observations about the nature of their role. Or you could allude to some piece of gossip about the industry. An example might start:

> I was at the Technology in Structural Engineering convention the other week and met a couple of procurement managers there, which reminded me of you. They said that the biggest problem they face at the moment is …

An email might then go on to suggest: "I don't know whether you are facing the same issues, but meeting them made me think of you."

It almost does not matter what reason you use to get in touch – so long as there is a genuine reason for doing so. Every month or so, I take a few minutes to peruse my list of contacts and think about people I have not been in touch with, and excuses that I might use to send them an email or pick up the telephone.

If you hear that your contact has been promoted, received an honor or award, or changed job, that would constitute a very good reason to get in touch – to congratulate them, make them feel good and, incidentally, remind them that you exist.

Equally, whenever anything newsworthy happens to you, this also provides you with an opportunity to pick up the telephone or compose an email. Job changes, promotions, new product launches, successfully hitting a major organizational milestone – all of these might be relevant if you can find a way to make it sound interesting to someone else.

Sports and activities outside of work could be legitimate reasons too. I don't follow football myself, but I know plenty of managers who email each other or send text messages to tease each other – good naturedly, I assume – when their team wins or the other person's team loses badly.

What else might work for you?

Build bridges

Networking is not just about getting more and more people into your list of contacts. One of the best ways to reinforce your relationship with one contact is to put them in touch with another person with whom they might have a mutual interest.

Building bridges between contacts is an ideal way to follow up as you are providing your contact with something useful – and incidentally reminding them that you not only exist, but are also thinking of them. By providing them with useful contacts, they will gradually become more and more grateful to you, until the time is right for when you might want to tap them for help.

Early last year, for instance, I was corresponding with the head of resourcing and development at a potential client organization. She mentioned that she was due to be made redundant from her job. I have some contacts in recruitment agencies and suggested that she get in touch with some of them. Even though she already knew two out of the three agencies, she was still grateful for the leads. Eight months on, she has found a new job and is now one of my clients.

As another example, I met Marissa Woods, an extremely good networker who runs Image Factor, a personal branding consultancy. We met and discussed what we both did. There have been no immediate opportunities to work together, but when I mentioned that I did a lot of work with professional services firms – accountants, bankers, and lawyers – she put me in touch with another contact of hers who was also doing some work with lawyers. Nothing has come of the opportunity so far, but now I feel that I am obliged to return the favor.

When introducing people to each other, as a matter of courtesy do mention it to both parties that you will be putting them in touch. You could copy them in on the same email, providing them with each other's contact details.

Effective networking can be like matchmaking – putting people in touch with each other and hoping that they get together, get married, and have babies together.

Or, to put it into more professional language, hoping that they meet, strike a deal, and manage to do business. So who in your contact list might be ready to walk up the aisle together?

Hanging on the telephone

Short of turning up at someone's workplace, nothing is more immediate than making a phone call. At the same time though, phone calls can be a distraction or at worst a downright annoyance if you have no good reason for getting in touch.

Make sure you have something worthwhile to say. It is not good enough to interrupt someone's day only to chat. Do you have something to say that simply could not wait or be dealt with by email? For example, many journalists use the phone to gather quotes for articles as opposed to using email because they are working to a deadline. That, to me, is a good enough reason.

It might be that you have an opportunity to share with the other person that is too complex to explain by email. Or perhaps it is sensitive and you would rather not commit it to electronic perpetuity.

Whatever your reason, make sure that you introduce yourself properly. You may have made diligent notes and kept tabs on them, but the likelihood that they have done the same on you is small. Begin with your name and a sentence reminding them how they know you. "Hi, it's Rob Yeung from Talentspace here. We met at the Learning Technologies conference at Olympia back in January."

Continue by asking if the person has a moment to talk. "Do you have a few minutes to talk right now?" If they are busy, ask them when would be a good time to call back.

Only when you have checked that they are not busy should you go on to make your suggestion or provide your piece of information.

After delivering your message, follow the other person's lead as to whether to continue the conversation or hang up. Do they sound as if they are rushing to finish the call? If they make little comment or ask you no questions about yourself, thank them for their time and hang up. Only if they engage you with questions about yourself should you allow the conversation to wander.

In rare cases when the other person is talking for too long – perhaps you have a meeting to go to or another call to make – try the following to end the conversation: "I'm conscious of your time. I don't want to take any more of your time so I should leave you alone now." It makes you sound as if you are trying to look after them rather than get rid of them.

Stand and deliver

How many times have you been on the telephone and indicated to a colleague that you are bored by rolling your eyes or pretending to yawn? The content of a phone call – what you say – is important, but it is only part of the message. The tone of your voice – how you say your message – is just as important.

I sometimes work from home and say to colleagues that it is a good thing that videophones haven't caught on yet. One of the joys of working from home is that you don't need to shave, comb your hair, or wear your best outfit. But before I pick up the telephone I always make the effort to smile – to plant a smile on my face even if I don't feel particularly inclined to do so. I know some people who also stand up when taking phone calls, as if they are giving a formal presentation.

Why? Because researchers (yes, psychologists again) have found that callers can discern a surprising amount about our mood from our tone of voice.

When we behave as if we are happy and pleased to be speaking to someone, this transmits down the telephone line. If we slump over our desks, the other person can detect our lack of energy too.

Even when we are leaving a voicemail rather than speaking with the person, our voice betrays more about us than we may expect. Some people not only stand while they speak but also use their free hand to make gestures as if they were presenting to an audience, as it too helps them to communicate their passion and dynamism more effectively.

Become e-ffective

Four quick tips for effective email networking.

First, use your subject line. Too many people I know leave it blank or use a bland word such as "meeting," "hello," or "thanks." Don't oversell by implying that something is urgent when it is not. But try to come up with something a little more inspired.

Second, don't bombard people with jokes, movie clips, and stories. Most people don't have the time for them – and the payoff is rarely worth the effort you put into reading them. If you come across an item that is of specific rele. vance to a particular person, that's fine. Only today, a contact of mine sent me a web link to a survey of the worst mistakes that candidates have ever made in interviews. It was relevant because a big chunk of my job is to do with interviewing people. If you do decide to send anything amusing, always forward it with a short message explaining your rationale for sending it to them.

Third, learn how to add a signature to the bottom of your outgoing emails. At the very least add your contact details so that people know your postal address and mobile number. Your website address should also go on it. Or, if you don't already have one, how about a short statement about what your business does?

The final and biggest tip is not to become over-reliant on email. Even amongst hi-tech firms, people feel compelled to do business in the distinctly no-tech manner of getting together in person. For example, US Cellular, an American wireless phone company, introduced a rule last year banning email on Fridays in an attempt to give employees what they wanted – the opportunity to speak with colleagues and customers rather than exchange impersonal missives on screen.

Email is high-tech, but low-touch – and can never replace the no-tech, high-touch interaction of meeting up.

Press the flesh

The rather odious saying "to press the flesh" conjures up slightly unsavory mental images. But thousands of years of evolution mean that, as human beings, we respond to being able to see each other, hear each other, and touch each other. That's why we still shake hands when we meet. Many cultures go even further and embrace or kiss each other on the cheeks when they meet – and that includes the men.

We also talk about seeing "eye to eye," which implies that eye contact is a prerequisite to building trust. There are elements of rapport and relationship building that can only be gained by meeting and spending time with each other.

No matter how busy we are, we all need social contact. And if you have a good enough reason to get in touch, people will make the time to see you.

Setting up a meeting at someone's office sends a clear message that you want a formal discussion. The signal you are sending is that the meeting is predominantly about business – perhaps to make an official request or to try to broker a deal.

If, however, you are interested more in building the relationship, then suggest meeting outside of the office, perhaps for a coffee break, a breakfast meeting, lunch, or a drink after work. I know many networkers who pick up the telephone and say, "I have a meeting in your area and I was wondering if you might be free for a coffee/drink/sandwich" – despite the fact that they actually have no meetings but are secretly hoping to have one with that particular person.

Do consider the other person's time constraints, though. If you know that the end of the accounting year means that they are inundated with work, skip the lavish three-course lunch in favor of a quick coffee. Or might it be sensible to wait a few weeks?

For the more artistically minded networkers amongst you, there is also the option of taking guests to galleries, museums, and exhibitions. Many galleries and museums encourage visitors to pay to become members, which typically entitles them to invite guests to private viewings – the perfect opportunity to strengthen a relationship if you know that someone has an interest in the arts.

Or if a contact is not interested in the arts, might there be a sporting interest that you share? Golf is the archetypal businessperson's game, but I know plenty of people who have secured clients on the squash and tennis court too.

Whatever the setting, be sure to pay. Whether you are taking someone for a coffee and muffin at Starbucks or to see a Dali retrospective, if you made the suggestion to meet up, you are the host. No matter how strongly they may protest, do not allow your contact to split the bill with you.

Meeting up is the best way to strengthen relationships. Even if you do not need to meet with your contacts, you should make the effort to meet with them a couple of times a year – whenever possible – to keep the relationship alive. A meeting is worth a half-dozen emails and phone calls. At least once or twice a month, look through your list of contacts. Who would it benefit you to meet?

Networker or nuisance?

Ever been in love? Can't wait to get in touch with someone, think about them all the time, want to send them gifts, and be with them? That's exactly how Glenn Close's bunny boiler in *Fatal Attraction* felt. She didn't think that she was stalking Michael Douglas – she thought that she was in love.

Just as there is a fine line that can be crossed from being a persistent romantic to becoming an obsessive stalker, there is a fine line that distinguishes being a diligent networker from making a nuisance of yourself. It is entirely possible that someone is busy and forgets to return your call. Perhaps they have your email in their inbox and do appreciate hearing from you, but have not had the time to reply. But it is just as possible that they find you bothersome and are too polite to tell you to leave them alone.

A colleague of mine, Clare, once coached a manager to help him develop his presentation skills – to be more charismatic and entertain an audience. The manager was very pleased with the coaching, and kept in touch afterwards. He corresponded with Clare by email and phoned her for advice. Now, he probably thought that a phone call once every couple of weeks was okay. But it was not okay, and Clare nicknamed him "turd," because he was like the lingering smell you get when you have stepped on something.

It's a very easy line to cross. And, especially if you have nothing of immediate interest to offer someone, persistence quickly turns into nuisance.

The motto "third time lucky" serves as my guide. If I get ignored once or twice, I assume that they might be busy, forgot to return my call, or deleted my email by mistake. I usually make a note in my list of contacts about each attempt that I make – so that I avoid repeating myself by accident. For example: "Emailed 20 June re: Recruitment Society summer party – no reply. Phoned and left voicemail 28 June – no reply."

Of course, if they do reply, I amend my notes to mention what their response was. But if I don't manage to speak to them or get a reply on the supposedly lucky third time, then I take it for granted that they are not interested. It does not mean that you need to delete them from your list of contacts, although you might want to make a note not to get in touch for the time being.

Do persevere; don't stalk.

Respond to requests

Congratulate yourself when people start to ask you for help. It is a sign that your efforts are paying off. For every request that you help with, you are banking a favor until you are ready to get help too.

However, it is possible to be too helpful. There are only 24 hours in a day, and I assume that you need to sleep for a handful of those hours. You need to be slightly selfish and think about what might be in it for you. Keep an eye on the cost/benefit ratio. On the cost side of the equation, how much time or energy and effort will it take you to respond to their request? And on the benefit side, if you do succeed in helping with the request, how thankful will they be to you?

If the costs significantly outweigh the benefits, then you may have to let the other person know that you won't be able to help them. If you can live with it, you could tell a white lie about how busy you are.

Also, bear in mind that some of the people who ask for our help may not be the kind of people who are ever likely to be of help to us. I call them "vampires" – people who drain our time and energy without providing much in return.

One such category of vampires are competitors. Especially if you run your own business or work freelance, you will inevitably run into people who provide similar services. If they are also seeking new clients, you must be realistic and con.sider that you may never get anything useful out of them.

On the other hand, it is useful to know a few. They can be a useful source of news and gossip about the industry or the market. Just keep in mind the cost/benefit ratio of keeping in touch with them. People in non-competing industries are more likely to refer job opportunities or work to you.

Another category of vampires are individuals who are very much more junior than us – perhaps on the lookout for career advice and support. Our every word may be useful to them, but being realistic, what sorts of favors are we ever likely to ask of them? And if they are very much more junior, is it likely that they would spontaneously recommend us to anyone of influence?

No one can lay down ironclad rules for who you should or should not help, who you should or should not stay in touch with. You are intelligent enough to be able to evaluate when, who, and how to help. Just don't be too helpful – look after your own interests too.

Hot or not

As the months and years roll by, your contacts list will swell and grow. Dozens of contacts will turn into hundreds, and hundreds into thousands. It can all become too much to keep track of.

And that is why I keep a "hot list" of key contacts – people that I think are of particular importance. Who makes it onto your hot list depends on what your objective is. Perhaps they have expressed an interest in buying your services – they might not have the need right now, but it might be worth keeping track of them until they do have such a need. Maybe you are looking for a job and have established that they are very well connected in your field. Or even if you don't have an objective at the moment, you may have the foresight to realize that this is a senior and/or influential person who might be able to help you in the future.

My hot list tends to be around 20 to 30 people – I find that I can't keep track of more people effectively. But your list may start with only two or three people. Or it may expand to 50 or 60. Just make sure that you genuinely can keep track of and in touch with however many you choose.

I copy out their details into a separate document and keep tabs on them in the following way:

Name	Previous activity	Future activity

Once people are on the list, I print out the list once a month and think about what I could do to get in touch with people. For example, asking selected contacts to contribute to this book was a good way to offer them something – an opportunity to get their names in print and raise their profiles.

On the following page is an example of the kind of notes that have helped me:

Name	Previous activity	Future activity
John Anonymous, HR Director of Zebra Marketing	• Was introduced to him through Peter Marks. Met 7 June for informal chat about Zebra's goals and my services • Emailed *Sunday Times* article on recruitment 10 June as follow up. • Emailed him 29 August offering a free copy of personality test to complete • Posted him copy of *Guardian* letter to editor on recruitment problems in marketing businesses, 8 October • Emailed him and Peter Marks 21 November to invite them to contribute to networking book – they replied suggesting colleague Jessica Hall	• Need to email in January to set up a meeting in Feb/March to see how their restructuring is going. Any opportunities? • Maybe put him in touch with Emma Maitland, HR Director of OIC Communications?

Use the grapevine

Gossip, gossip. Whisper, whisper. Everyone hears rumors and stories on the grapevine. It is natural for people getting together to talk about other people that they have in common, especially if they work in a similar industry that allows their paths to cross frequently.

You will hear news both good and bad. There may be life events such as marriages, anniver.saries, births and other celebrations as well as divorces, illnesses, and deaths. People move houses, their children pass exams, and their personal lives go through peaks and troughs. At work, there may be news of job transitions, successes, or widely publicized difficulties.

Such events can often be opportunities to get in touch to congratulate or commiserate with oth.ers. However, do be careful to check that your information is correct. Famously, on reading his own obituary, Mark Twain once commented, "Rumors of my death are greatly exaggerated."

Stories are often inadvertently distorted by lapses of memory or repeated retelling, and sometimes intentionally twisted to sensationalize and make a greater impact. Take the time to quiz your contacts to ensure that you are hearing a genuine item of news rather than a rumor.

Consider also whether the person at the center of the news would want others to know of their news. People are proud of weddings and promo.tions. But would they want others to know that they have been made redundant?

Use your judgment before picking up the telephone or composing an email.

The Z-list

As your main contacts list grows and grows, you may be tempted to remove people from it. Certainly, if you have tried to make contact a couple of times but not heard anything, you should give up rather than risk pestering them. After several years, it would be very natural to want to remove them from your list – especially if you keep your list of contacts in paper form on note cards or in a Rolodex.

Rather than discarding them entirely, why not remove them to a separate Z-list? Or the beauty of keeping your list in electronic form rather than on paper is that you never need delete anyone. It doesn't take up physical space, so why not leave them be?

Again, it's a lesson I have learnt from bitter experience. Six years ago, I researched web designers to find one to revamp the website of the consultancy that I used to work for, and I found one who did a very good job. But when I left that consultancy, I pruned my contacts list and removed people that I deemed no longer relevant. Guess what? A few months ago, I met a potential client who was asking for recommendations of good website designers. If I had kept the designer's details, I would have had the perfect reason for following up.

Don't delete anyone. Separate them into different lists if you want. But if you intend to be in business for the long run, just about everyone could eventually become relevant.

Why Christmas is a waste of time …

Before I get letters of complaints from people, I am not implying that Christmas itself is a waste of time. But, contrary to what many networking gurus advocate, I do think that Christmas is the worst time of year to try to make an impact on people.

Certainly, as you meet more and more people, you will find yourself being added to their Christmas mailing lists and receiving more and more cards each year. And you may find yourself having to reply to their Christmas missives out of politeness. But it is not a good time to try to make an impact because we all receive so many cards.

You could try to compose a message that is pithy and interesting. But your message may only get a cursory glance if someone has a dozen other cards to open that morning. If you are sending a card to a senior person, your card may get opened by an assistant and put on a shelf without reaching the person you intended to contact.

Business etiquette dictates that you send Christmas cards, but don't waste time trying to personalize messages. Write the same message in all of them. "Dear X. Best wishes for the festive season and look forwards to catching up in the new year, Rob."

An alternative is not to send cards at all. Some businesses instead donate to charity the money that they would have spent on postage and having cards printed, and inform clients and contacts of this fact by email.

Save your energies for the rest of the year when everyone else has nothing to send.

… But birthdays are not

I know a freelance television producer who is always on the lookout for his next piece of work. Contracts can last for as little as a few months, and rarely for longer than six or eight months. So at least once or twice a year, he has to go through a process of finding a new job.

But he shared his secret with me:

> I keep a record of everyone's birthdays – or at least all of the executive producers who might be able to offer me a new gig. At the start of the year, I buy a big stack of inoffensive birthday cards. And I make sure that I send one to each of my contacts when their birthday comes round. Grown-ups just don't get birthday cards, so they always remember me when I'm next looking for a job.

Not a bad tip, eh?

05

Put your Network to Work

Rapport is an intangible concept. You can't see it or quantify it, but you will know when you have it. The time will come when you have built up suf.ficient rapport and banked enough favors to ask for help. Perhaps it is to help you find a job, gain introductions to new customers, or raise money for a new business venture or your favorite cause.

The good news is that you have already done the hard bit. Meeting people and establishing a network takes time and dedication. Asking for help is much more straightforward. And this is how to do it.

Focus your objective

Way back near the beginning of the book, we talked about establishing an objective, because it is useful to have a general sense of why you are networking. Now that you have worked on building up your network, it's time to think about how to achieve your objective.

It is always a mistake to be too specific when networking. I deliberately avoided suggesting at the start of the book setting a specific objective because, when meeting people, it helps to think broadly rather than too narrowly. Say you have a product that is aimed at left-handed atheists who drink champagne on Saturday evenings after 9 pm. If you go out with the mindset of wanting to meet only left-handed atheists who drink cham.pagne on Saturday evenings after 9 pm – well, that's too restricted a market, you're never going to find many of them, and will only be disap.pointed by the whole process of networking. However, going out there to look for people who might be willing to talk about your product – that is a very different issue, and is much more likely to net you some left-handed atheists who drink champagne on Saturday evenings after 9 pm.

But now that you have started to establish a network and have followed up with them a number of times, you may be ready to think about how best to ask them for help.

Before you can go speak to people, you first need to define your objective in greater detail. If, for example, you are looking for a job, what exactly are you looking for? Are you looking for more responsibility and a bigger salary? Or is that less important than a different culture that fits you better? Perhaps you want to move out of one industry sector or retrain in an entirely different field. In order to ask people for help, you need to be able to articulate not only what you want, but why you want it.

To take another example, if you are trying to raise support for a charity, what form should it take? Which would you prefer – for them to give you cash or for them to give you their time? Are there other alternatives – for example could they make an endowment in their will? And why is the charity important? What does the charity do? What is unique about it?

Remember that you are the expert on your own objective – others are unlikely to understand the background without you telling it to them. If you are not able to explain clearly, then what hope do you have of persuading them?

Ask and you shall receive

When I started networking, I used to be afraid to ask for what I wanted. Despite building good relationships with people, I used to balk at making requests because I thought it might ruin the relationship. I did not want to appear crass; I did not want people to think that I couldn't succeed on my own. But the moment I started asking contacts for support – to get a job, to help find new clients – people were almost immediately helpful.

When I asked one contact, he even said to me: "I've always enjoyed our lunches, Rob, but I'd been wondering for quite a long time when you were going to ask if you could do business with our business."

As long as you are have taken some steps to develop a good relationship, then ask. If someone can help, they almost certainly will. But they are not telepathic – they can't read your mind. You need to speak up.

Consider what medium to use – email, phone, or face-to-face – for your request. As a rule of thumb, straightforward requests are fine by email. But more complex, demanding, or challenging requests need to be made over the telephone or face-to-face. By email, share some of your news first. By telephone, allow a minute or two for pleasantries before launching into your request.

Personally, my preferred option is to email ahead with my request and then to end the email by saying that I will call in a couple of days' time to see if they have any thoughts on the matter. If I know that someone is difficult to get hold of, I often also add, "Let me know when would be a good time to call." Then I make damn sure that I do call.

When you do speak, keep your initial request succinct and unambiguous. Asking, "Do you know anyone who might be able to help me grow my business?" is vague – it could equally imply that you are looking for a consultant to help you analyze your business or that you are looking for new customers. But asking, "Do you know any organizations that might need our services?" will leave others in no doubt as to what you are looking for.

Some examples:

- "As you know, we are a design consultancy. Would you know the right person to speak with in your organization to discuss whether there might be opportunities to work together?"
- "I'm currently looking for a job as a sales manager in the media sector. Would you know anyone who might be able to help? Either a contact in HR or recruitment or perhaps someone who can give me any advice."
- "We have more work than we can handle. Would you know of any good engineers who might want to join us?"

As long as the request is not offensive, most people feel flattered to receive requests for help. Be direct. If they can help, you may be able to secure your ultimate objective.

Ask, and you shall receive.

Getting past no

In many cases, no matter how well-phrased your request, the other person's initial answer will be "No." Not because they don't want to help, but because they can't immediately think of anyone who might be able to help with your request. Especially if you telephone them without having given them prior warning by email, people often struggle to come up with ideas. They need your help to think about how to help you.

Think about ways to facilitate the discussion – to provide them with prompts to encourage them to think more broadly about your request. Otherwise the conversation may be painfully short.

A networker looking for new clients might prompt with the following chain of questions:

- "Would you know the name and number of the right person to speak to within your organization?"
- "No? Do you at least know the right department that I should be speaking to? Do you know anyone within that depart.ment that I could call? If I could speak to them and mention your name, they might be able to help."

If you have been diligently building the relationship, you should also know a considerable amount about each person that you speak to. Where else have they worked? What associations do they belong to? Have they ever mentioned other people that you could speak to? If the first few questions fail to draw a response, use further prompts such as:

- "What about outside your organization? You used to work for Australian Steel. Would you know the person I might be able to speak to there? Or would you have any old contacts still in that business that might be able to point me in the right direction?"

- "I met you back in January at the annual conference of the Print and Broadcast Journalism Society. Do you go to any other events? Have you met any people at those events that might be able to help?"

If they continue to struggle to come up with ideas, you may want to give them further time to think: "I realize that you may not be able to come up with any suggestions immediately. When would be a good time to call back?"

Rarely does networking allow you to achieve your objective in a single step. More often that not, you will need to contact someone who may know someone who knows somebody else who can put you in touch with the person you need. Remember the theory about "six degrees of separation," and those experiments by Stanley Milgram? It is important for you to keep this in mind – but doubly important for you to impress this fact upon your contacts.

Otherwise your con.tacts may feel disheartened that they cannot give you the name and number of the exact person you are looking for. Explain that you will need to work through a long chain of contacts to achieve your objective. Encourage them by telling them that if they can give you the name of just one person to speak to – no matter how unlikely the lead – they are helping you to get closer to your objective.

Networking is about taking not a single bound but many small steps to reach your objective.

The people who know the people you know

If a stranger rang you today and asked you for help, you would probably first be slightly perplexed as to how they got your details. Perhaps you might demand how they got your number and then you would put the phone down on them. You might also be either fairly curt or downright angry with them for wasting your time.

Now consider if someone rang you and named someone you know very well who had suggested you would be able to help. Immediately, the mention of a name you recognize is almost certain to make you want to listen to the stranger on the other end of the telephone. You would give them at least a few minutes of your time, wouldn't you?

Given that our immediate circle of contacts is never as large as we would like, it is inevitable that we will eventually need to get in touch with the contacts of our contacts – people that we have never spoken to before. To them, we are little more than strangers.

The way you introduce yourself to them makes all the difference to whether they decide to help you or hang up on you.

The ideal approach is to ask the person that you do know to get in touch with their contact on your behalf. All it takes is a short phone call or email from them mentioning your name so that when you get in touch, you will not get ignored. If your contact needs help wording an email, then something along the lines of the following may be enough:

> Dear Sarah. I hope you are well. I've been working with Rob Yeung, who runs a business psychology consultancy. He is on the lookout for clients who may be interested in using his consultancy for assessment or development services. I suggested that you might be able to point him in the right direction of people to speak to on this matter. If you could spare him a few minutes of your time, I would be most grateful.

If you ask your contact to send the email to the intended recipient ("Sarah" in this case) and to copy you in on the email, it is then a simple matter for you to get in touch with the recipient directly.

You could then send a short email with some more detail about the precise nature of your request, and make a phone call a few days later to introduce yourself properly and explain the context to your request.

Make sure that you are unfailingly polite in your conversation. After all, your demeanor with this new person reflects on the person who provided the introduction. If you are at all inconsiderate of their time or unwittingly rude, how likely is it that your contact will ever again introduce you to anyone else?

Script your dialog

Whether you are having a telephone conversation or a face-to-face meeting, you can help yourself to make the discussion as effective as possible by writing a script for what you intend to say.

People are busy and you need to make the best use of the limited time that you have available with them. Treat a script as a summary of points that you should aim to cover. A good script should cover the five "i"s:

- *Identification.* How are you going to identify yourself or tell the other person who you are? If it is an existing contact and you have not been in touch for quite a while, do you need to recap how you met? If you have never had any dealings with this person, do you need a short explanation of how you came to know the person who put the two of you in touch? Do you need to provide a brief description of what you do?
- *Icebreaking.* Spend a couple of minutes building rapport. People hate feeling that they are being used. Even if you are only getting in touch because you need something from them, it is one of the unwritten rules

of networking that you must appear that you are not getting in touch only because you need something from them. You know the truth. And they know the truth too, but it is good manners for you both to pretend otherwise. That's just how it is. So what questions will you ask or topics will you discuss before launching into your request?

- *Introductions.* If you need to ask for a referral onto other people that they know, then how will you phrase your request? Who or what exactly do you need? Why do you need it? And how will it help you?

- *Information gathering.* Not everyone will be able to provide you with introductions to further people. Sometimes, the best use of someone's time is not in making them think of people that may be able to help you, but in sharing the knowledge or information that they possess. For example, a headhunter could provide you with contacts within employers, or could provide you with an overview of the job market. A market analyst might know people who might be willing to invest, but perhaps it would be a better use of your one phone conversation or meeting to find out what they know about the marketplace and the potential for your product.

- *Impression.* Finally, what impact or impression do you want to leave with each person you encounter? Of course you want to build a rapport with everyone you come across – in case you should want to get in touch again. If you know anything at all about their personality or interests beforehand, try to adopt a demeanor that will allow you to connect with them. Are they business-like and professional, or informal and chatty? Are they driven by examples and experience, or interested in exploring concepts and ideas? Are they more interested in facts and figures, or feelings and emotions? People like people who are like themselves. So, for the purposes of this one discussion, how can you be more like them?

I'm not saying that you must stick to your script no matter what. In fact, good networkers must be prepared to deviate from the script, depending on how the contact responds and directs the flow of the conversation. However, having a good idea in your own mind of what you want to say will help you to sound more articulate. It may sound like a contradiction in terms, but you should prepare thoroughly in order to sound spontaneous.

Put pen to paper, again

I cannot emphasize enough how important it is to thank your contacts for every conversation or exchange of information you have with them. No matter how trivial their help actually turned out to be, take the time to thank them.

Just because you have written them one handwritten note in the process of building the relationship does not mean that you cannot do it again. Precisely because rapport and relationships are so intangible, a handwritten note acts as a very tangible, physical manifestation of your gratitude.

Yes, you may feel that you have now established a sufficient level of rapport to be able to rely on email, phone calls, or even face-to-face meetings. But in the world of work, we expect to receive emails and phone calls and to meet with people in person. We don't expect – and are therefore pleasantly surprised by – handwritten notes.

If you take away just one point from this book, begin to send thank you notes written by hand.

And no, it does not count if you ask your assistant to write it out by hand.

Reveal your hidden circle of contacts

When asked to list the people in their network, most aspiring networkers consider only their business contacts. But the fact is that our business contacts form only a small part of our total circle of contacts.

If you are serious about wanting to achieve your objective, then you should consider that almost every single person (apart from, possibly, children) you know is a contact – a person who might know someone who knows somebody else who might be able to further your pursuit of your objective.

A useful exercise is to make a list of everyone that you know. Yes, everyone. It will take a while, but it will be worth the effort.

Begin by thinking about the many spheres of your life that you inhabit. At work, think about people in your current organization and previous organizations. Think about ex-colleagues – bosses, peers, and people who reported to you – who have moved on to other organizations too. How about suppliers and customers both past and present?

Outside of your work, think about your family and friends. What about people you know from school, college, university, and other educational establishments? How about sports clubs, voluntary associations, or community groups? What about your bank manager and other financial advisors? Military service or religious organizations? Even neighbors that you are on friendly terms with?

It doesn't matter what form your list takes. Some people like to draw spider diagrams or "mind maps" that radiate out from a central point. Others like to draw up tables with different headings at the top of each column:

Current business	Previous business	Family	School friends	College friends	Evening class	Tennis club	Church	Etcetera ...

The key here is to be as comprehensive as possible – list everyone that you are on speaking terms with as well as everyone that you think you could possibly bear to get in touch with again. Don't assume that anyone may not be important. While you may be tempted to leave someone off the list because you think they are unlikely to be able to contribute directly in helping you to reach your objective, how can you know for certain that they couldn't introduce you to people who can help you with your objective?

Then begin getting in touch with people from your list – using all of the skills and techniques that are covered in Chapter 2, "Build your network, one person at a time."

Never approach someone and reveal your objective straightaway – especially if you are trying to get a job or sell something. Linda Caller, managing director of consultancy Thought Agents, relates:

> Alan and I worked closely in the same organization for five years. He left to pursue pastures new, and we lost touch. A year later he called me out of the blue. I was delighted he'd found me again, until he explained he had called to sell me a financial services package.
>
> My spirit dropped and my heart hardened. Maybe, just maybe, he had identified a financial product that was just right for me. But no, I felt I was being used – I was just a sales target despite everything we'd been through together. So what happened next? After his follow-up call I didn't call him. He didn't call me, and we have never communicated again.

Getting to the stage of being able to use your hidden circle of contacts is a time-consuming process, and you need to be diligent in taking notes to ensure that you can keep track of which people you have already spoken to, and who has referred you to whom. Take into account how you know them, and the nature of your relationship. Always begin an email or telephone call by mentioning in passing whatever you have in common with them.

It is tempting to go through all of your current and previous work contacts in an effort to avoid approaching your social contacts. But given the unpredictability of networking – we can never say who might know someone useful – a better strategy is to try a handful from every sphere of your life. With your friends and family, you already have a strong bond, so why wouldn't they want to help you out?

Further your career

A modern-day adage says that we should "work smart, not hard." Indeed, hard work and good results by themselves are not enough to guarantee career success. The people who succeed not only produce results, but also ensure that others know about their good work, by creating a profile for themselves too. Having lots of people know you and like you will put you in good stead when it comes to handing out promotions, or thinking of people to put onto interesting new projects.

But one of the best ways to further your career is to seek a career mentor. Whether you work within a large organization or work for yourself, you can seek a mentor. Even better, have one mentor within your organization and another outside it.

"Your network is part of your career development, so approach people who are where you would like to be. Ask them what you need to do to get onto the radar," advises Suzanne Wood, a partner at leading headhunting firm Heidrick & Struggles.

You can realize your career goals much more quickly by enlisting the support of someone who has already achieved what you want. Look for someone within your organization who has reached or surpassed the career steps that you want to take. Avoid choosing someone who is too many steps ahead of you on the career ladder, as they may not want to mentor someone too junior. And ensure that it is someone that you respect and can see yourself spending time with, as you must be willing to listen to his or her advice, even though at times it may go counter to what you feel to be right.

If you can't find someone within your organiza.tion, or perhaps you want a mentor both within and outside of your organization, then ask your network for suggestions. Who might understand your industry or profession enough to instruct and guide you? Mentors need not be based in the same geographic location as you. Advice can be as easily dispensed down a telephone as in person.

Before approaching a prospective mentor, make sure that you can define your career objective. If you cannot explain it succinctly to a prospective mentor, why should they agree to take you on?

Approach a prospective mentor in the same way as any other contact. Perhaps by email or telephone, introduce yourself and explain that you would like to set up a short meeting or telephone conversation to explore whether they might be willing to enter into a mentoring relationship with you.

Mention in your initial message some of the positive reasons that you are seeking this person's advice – a little flattery rarely goes wrong. For example, the person may have achieved career success at a particularly young age, or may have a reputation within the industry.

If they say that they are too busy to take you on, then ask them whether they might be able to recommend a mentor. Then continue on your search. Don't expect to find a mentor immediately.

When you do meet or speak, be ready to answer their questions. Who are you? What do you want from the mentoring relationship? How will it work? When and how often would it happen? Where will it happen? Why should they do it?

Make the most of mentoring

Once you have persuaded a mentor to take you on as their "mentee," think about how to structure the relationship to suit you both.

For example, you might arrange a time slot every few weeks or months to talk over specific issues, explain current dilemmas, and seek advice. Or you might ask your mentor to let you shadow them doing parts of the job that you struggle with – perhaps making presentations, handling client negotiations, or running team meetings. Or you might ask them to share tips and tactics that have allowed them to succeed.

Mentoring can take many forms. Most people have different mentors to help them through different career stages, while some people have one mentor for the duration of their careers.

Some meet monthly for several hours, while others may arrange a half-hour conference call only quarterly. The only issue to bear in mind when arranging when and for how long to talk is to ensure that you respect their time. While you could argue that they benefit by developing their coaching skills, the reality is that mentoring is mainly a one-way relationship – you get most of the benefit. Treat their time as a valuable resource, and use it well. If you have scheduled a three-hour session but run out of topics to discuss usefully, then cut the discussion short. Or, ultimately, if the mentoring relationship ceases to be useful, then end it graciously rather than let it die a slow and lingering death.

Once you have experienced being mentored, you should also seek out opportunities to mentor others. Send the message out on your network that you are willing to mentor. It will develop your coaching skills, allow you to pass something on to the next generation, and help you to extend your network of contacts in a different direction. As you become more senior, mature, and experienced, your contacts will also tend to become more seasoned and responsible. But along with those positive traits, your contacts may also tend to become more set in their ways and less open-minded to new ideas and change. So mentoring younger people may help you to keep abreast of new developments, and allow you access to fresher ideas and more naïve perspectives.

Ask for a job, by not asking for a job

Networking your way into a new job is no different from any other form of networking. You must think through your objective. Are you looking for a new job in the same industry, or to change careers entirely? You need to think about how you introduce yourself to people. Then you need to create an elevator speech to sell yourself, and you must have short anecdotes ready to illustrate your key skills.

What you must never do when you are looking for a job, however, is appear too needy. People like to deal with other people who are happy and confident – they find it painful to be with people who appear desperate, or have a sense of hopelessness about them.

Never ask your contacts directly if they have got a job for you. Asking them for a job puts them on the spot. The answer will almost certainly be "No," and then you will struggle to take the conversation further.

The best way to open up conversations with your contacts is to ask them for advice or information. Always begin with the usual pleas.antries before going on to asking for advice. For example, someone looking to change industries might ask:

I'm thinking about moving out of the retail sector
into consumer goods. I'm trying to talk to people

who work in consumer goods or who might have done so in the past to understand what it's like. Can you think of anyone who might be able to spare me the time for a short telephone conversation?

I would continue by assuaging any unspoken concerns of theirs that you might pester their contacts for a job:

I should add that I'm not asking for a job. If you can think of anyone who might be able to talk to me, I will not be asking them for a job. At this point in time, I'm trying to understand more about the market and the opportunities that are available in that field.

As you progress with your networking, don't just ask for contacts. Ask for information. What is the culture of the field? What are the trends within the industry? Who are the major players in the area? Who are the main recruitment agencies in the sector? What are customers looking for? What are the main challenges for the industry? Think about the right questions that you should ask each person to help you understand more about your chosen field. All of this information will eventually allow you to impress when you are offered interviews.

Ask also for advice. Never send your CV or resumé without being asked for it. But explain your situation and ask what each of your contacts would suggest you do. What pitfalls do they think you might encounter? And how do they suggest you overcome them?

Inject reality into a job search

Don't expect the first person you ring to be able to put you in touch with the right person. Consider someone who currently works as a finance analyst who wants to move out of pharmaceuticals and into fashion retail. It's likely that the first contacts that a person makes may be in retail, but not fashion. Further efforts might put him or her in touch with people who work for a fashion retailer – perhaps people who may work in sales or marketing, human resources, or the supply chain. And it might take further rounds of networking to make contact with the finance team within that fashion retailer. In all likelihood, the finance team within this first fashion retailer may only be able to provide information and advice rather than a job. But they should also be able to provide further contacts to continue networking with.

Networking is not a magic potion, though. No matter how many people you speak to, you can't network your way from being a call center operator to being the chief executive. We all have constraints that may hold us back – such as lack of skills or experience, family commitments, and financial needs.

Another useful way to use your network is therefore to ask about these constraints. Rather than repeating the same questions about the market and what it is like to work in that industry, ask the one or two questions that you think may limit your opportunities. For example, "Given my family commitments and my mortgage, I'd struggle to work for a salary of less than £50,000. Is that realistic given my relative lack of experience?" Or, "My daughter is taking an exam next year and needs to stay in this school so we can't move from London. How might that hold me back?"

Networking takes time and patience. But there is a huge hidden market of jobs that are never advertised but filled by word of mouth and rec.ommendation alone. And networking will help you to find it.

Find your way to new clients

What do you do when you need a decorator or a builder to do some work on your home? Rather than pick up a business directory, most people would prefer to ask friends for recommendations.

The same is true for just about any other service – from financial advisors to dentists. If your objective is to look for new clients or customers, the process of networking is not much different from any other objective. You need to have a clear idea of what you and your business can do for other people. What is your elevator speech? And what is the handful of stories that you can tell to illustrate why anyone might buy your services?

Before you go looking for new customers, though, make sure that your current customers are 100 percent satisfied. If they are not happy, why would they want to recommend you?

Do you ask your existing customers whether they are entirely happy with the service you provide them? Canny businesses use a variety of methods, including telephone interviews and written surveys, to gather customers' views. You could issue a survey with as few as three questions:

- What was good about how we did business with you?
- What was bad about how we did business with you?
- How could we improve our service to you?

Some organizations survey their customers annually. But if you are only asking a few simple questions by telephone, a short email, or a written questionnaire, why not do it more frequently – say quarterly? And when your customers provide you with feedback, make sure that you act on it. Don't get defensive if your customers are critical – accept that your customers are entitled to feel the way they do. Channel your energies in a more useful direction: apologize for any mistakes or problems and then sort them out.

All of your current customers should also be on your hot list. Look for ways to build relationships with your existing customers so they think of you as a friend rather than merely a supplier. Rather than waiting to get in touch only because you need to, look for ways to demonstrate that you are getting in touch because you want to. Be interested in their lives outside of the services or products they buy from you. What are their interests, and what do you have in common? How can you make doing business with them enjoyable as opposed to purely transactional?

Only when you are satisfied that your existing customers are entirely happy should you try to network through them to other customers. Asking existing customers for referrals to new potential customers is one of the most powerful methods for acquiring new customers.

As with any other objective, start by emailing them or calling them to alert them to the fact that you are looking for referrals. And then several days later, call again or arrange to meet to ask for names and contact details.

Once you have the details of prospective customers, don't expect them to turn into transacting customers immediately. Often, they may not have a current need for your services. Or they may already have suppliers that they use. Many large organizations have preferred supplier lists that they may only review once a year or even every few years.

The paradox of selling is that success requires listening, not telling. Customers hate feeling that they are being sold to. They like to feel that it is their choice whether to buy or not. Spend your time with new contacts building the relationship, rather than telling them again and again your marketing messages. Don't keep reminding them what you do – people get tired of hearing it too many times. Instead, ask what you can do for them. Even if it has nothing to do with the services that you provide, your willingness to solve problems for them will put you in good stead for when they do choose to buy.

Networking your way to new customers is not something that happens overnight. But it costs much less than an advertising budget, and delivers better results too.

Partner to win customers

There is an indirect way to secure new customers too. Rather than networking to find customers who can buy your services, you could network to build relationships with contacts that work in similar, but non-competing, fields.

For example, the type of small business customer that needs the services of a banker might also need the services of a financial advisor and a corporate lawyer.

As another, more personal, example, I'm a business psychologist. Which means that I provide assessment and development services – designing assessment centers, interviewing candidates, and providing executive coaching. My paying client tends to be the HR director within organizations. But I don't know anything about pensions or pay practices, nor about disciplinary procedure, or health and safety legislation. So when an HR director mentions one of these other issues, it is an opportunity for me to build the relationship with them by introducing them to carefully selected partners who can help. At the same time, it wins me favors with my partners – who in turn feel obliged to recommend me to their clients.

Identifying key contacts to partner with is a win–win situation.

Look for contacts that work in complementary fields and bear in mind whether there might be opportunities to work together and provide referrals to each other.

In order to strengthen the relationship, you might also think about agreeing a reward or commission system to incentivize each other to provide referrals. It could be an informal arrangement such as taking the other person out for a lavish dinner, or buying a luxury gift for a referral that generates business. Or it could be a more formal system that rewards a percentage of the income that either of you make from a newly referred customer. There are no rules as to how such systems should work – only that it should be genuinely beneficial to both parties.

So who would it make sense for you to get together with?

Final Words

I wish I could wave a magic wand and transform people into expert networkers. For a start, I would be a multi-millionaire. Unfortunately though, it doesn't work that way. Networking takes effort, thought, and persistence.

You need to prepare and practice an elevator speech and stories to tell. You need to generate questions to ask at every new event you attend. You need to be diligent in taking notes about the people you meet. Writing notes by hand will win you favors, but it takes longer than sending emails. And maintaining your network takes constant thought – what can I do or say to each and every person in my network to keep them thinking of me?

But while it does require effort, that is also the good news – because it is a skill that can be learnt rather than an innate gift. So anyone can do it – if you just try. It doesn't matter how you begin your journey to become a master networker. Send an email to someone you haven't spoken to for a long time. Research a conference on the Internet to attend. Sign up to give a talk to your team. Just start. Do something, no matter how small.

As with any skill, we become more proficient the more we exercise it. Just as we had to take faltering steps when we learnt to walk as babies, your first attempts to network may feel clumsy. It won't come naturally to begin with. But with time, we learnt to walk. We can walk or skip, dance, or run – and all without thinking about it, suddenly it has become second nature. And that is how networking will eventually become to you too.

Good luck!

About the Author

Dr Rob Yeung is a director at leading business psyhology consultancy Talentspace, where he specialize in interviewing and assessing senior managers. He also coaches executives, particularly in the areas of leadership and charisma. He works with a wide range of organizations including investment banks, law and accountancy firms, airlines, and advertising and media business.

He has written nine books on management topics and is often asked to contribute to print media including the *Guardian* and *Financial Times* as well as broadcast media including CNN.

A business school lecturer and frequently requested conference speaker, he is also the presenter of a highly acclaimed BBC television series on job hunting.

Books in the Business Solutions Series

BRILLIANT COMMUNICATION
5 steps to communicating your message clearly and effectively |
Patrick Forsyth

EFFECTIVE DECISION MAKING
10 steps to better decision making and problem solving | Jeremy
Kourdi

ESSENTIAL TIME MANAGEMENT
How to become more productive and effective | Brett Hilder

FAQS ON MARKETING
Answers and advice by the guru of marketing | Philip Kotler

GREAT NEGOTIATING SKILLS
The essential guide to getting what you want | Bob Etherington

GREAT SELLING SKILLS
How to sell anything to anyone | Bob Etherington

HOW TO MAKE A DIFFERENCE
Discover your purpose in life and change things for the better |
Tim Drake

MANAGE YOUR BOSS
How to create the ideal working relationship | Patrick Forsyth

MANAGING IN THE DISCOMFORT ZONE:
How to deal with sensitive, difficult and unpleasant situations |
Patrick Forsyth

MY BOSS IS A BASTARD!
Overcoming the boss from hell | Richard Maun

NEW JOB SURVIVAL KIT
10 steps to surviving and thriving in the first 100 days of your new job | Frances Kay

SIMPLY A GREAT MANAGER
The fundamentals of being a successful manager | Mike Hoyle & Peter Newman

SURVIVING OFFICE POLITICS
Coping and succeeding in the workplace jungle | Patrick Forsyth

THE NEW RULES OF ENTREPRENEURSHIP
What it really takes to become a savvy and successful entrepreneur | Rob Yeung

THE NEW RULES OF EQ
Using emotional intelligence to get ahead | Rob Yeung

THE NEW RULES OF JOBHUNTING
A modern guide to finding the job you want | Rob Yeung

THE NEW RULES OF NETWORKING
The essential rules and secrets to modern networking | Rob Yeung

WHY ENTREPRENEURS SHOULD EAT BANANAS
101 inspirational ideas for growing your business and yourself | Simon Tupman